SECOND CHANCES DON'T GROW ON TREES

PATRICK J MCLAUGHLIN

Matador
Unit E2 Airfield Business Park,
Harrison Road, Market Harborough,
Leicestershire. LE16 7UL
Tel: 0116 2792299
Email: books@troubador.co.uk
Web: www.troubador.co.uk/matador
Twitter: @matadorbooks

ISBN 978 1803131 313

British Library Cataloguing in Publication Data.
A catalogue record for this book is available from the British Library.

Printed and bound in Great Britain by 4edge Limited
Typeset in 11pt Minion Pro by Troubador Publishing Ltd, Leicester, UK

Matador is an imprint of Troubador Publishing Ltd

For Beverley, without whose support and encouragement
this book would not have seen the light of day.

ONE

Of course, there is no good time to have a heart attack. But this one could not have been worse timed. Today I should be starting a new job which could be life-changing. Instead, here I am, lying in a hospital bed in an intensive care ward, awaiting the visit of the consultant with his little flotilla of white-coated medical acolytes who will determine my future.

I had taken early retirement five years before after a career in education which had had its moments of sublimity but which had ended acrimoniously when my employers, the education department of the Edinburgh City Council, and I decided that we had had enough of each other.

The basic source of contention between us centred on our differing ideas of what constitutes education. I saw it as a catholic concept, that is all-encompassing and all-inclusive. It had to be for everyone and had to comprise the full range of their needs and interests, including their emotional and spiritual development, their growth in their own skins to emancipation. Mine was, in every sense, a child-centred approach.

The bureaucratic model that dominated formal education at that time, and still does to an even greater extent today, was all about passing more and more exams and getting higher and higher marks in the process. I had total contempt for this, measuring-obsessed, model of education which created elitism in the schools and the too-brisk dismissal of those with no aptitude or appetite for this form of corrupting competitiveness.

One dreadful consequence of all this can be seen in the very large number of pupils who leave school without having attained even basic levels in literacy and numeracy. The heavy concentration on success at an academic level and the apparently serene acceptance of failure on the part of those who are not academically gifted has the effect of devaluing the educational needs of the majority of pupils in our schools whose skills and ambitions point in other directions.

There is something I have always called 'being good-at-school'. It is one of the many individual gifts people have, like being good-looking, or artistic, or sporty, or simply being blessed with a kind and compassionate nature.

Being 'good-at-school' is a very specific form of giftedness but, oh, how it dominates in the school system. If you have it, it is the doorway to a world of opportunities in higher education, both in school and beyond. If you don't have it, then, no matter how accomplished you may be in other respects, the door remains closed to you, perhaps for ever.

And yet, in truth, this is a very restricted, and even pernicious, sort of talent. It leads to conformism and a too-willing deference to people in authority whose approval you crave at any price. You quickly find ways to succeed in exams and this becomes the be-all and end-all of your education. Furthermore, to perpetuate this folly, the exams become ever more restrictive and designed only to test what lends itself to testing; to the exclusion of those elements that are more subjective, more problematic and, ultimately, more estimable. More damaging still is the fact that the pupil's energies are consumed in working out what answer the teacher expects rather than the free exploration of the topic.

In my, perhaps unkind, disdain of academic high flyers I find comfort in the support of none other than that giant of literary criticism, the great F R Leavis. During his tenure as professor at Cambridge University he was, understandably, a magnet for the most ambitious post-graduates in pursuit of a PhD.

However, he was famously selective about who he allowed onto his doctoral programme and refused to consider anyone, except in the most exceptional circumstances, who attained first-class honours in their original degree. He did this because he considered such people to be in general a bad bet. All too often, he discovered, their academic success was the result of sheer hard work and shrewd calculation rather than feeling and imagination.

Does this sound familiar?

Let us return at this point to the secondary school setting and the formulaic and soulless assessment of

English language. This leads, among other things, to an excessive emphasis on the comparatively low-level clerical skills of writing; on punctuation and spelling. The assessment of these skills is easy. Much easier than the assessment of meaning and imagination. Important as these skills are, both operationally and personally, they are not top order skills and should not be the determining factor when judging a piece of writing.

The nonsense of the current upside-down emphasis on these clerical skills can be seen to be ridiculous when you consider the much freer punctuation system and the great number of variant spellings that were happily used by Shakespeare and the magnificent Elizabethan writers generally. It can also be seen in the large number of great writers in world literature who were poor spellers. Dostoevsky was, apparently, a famously bad speller. In a single poem W B Yeats, in a first draft, managed to misspell the same word three times – in three different ways! Of course, it did not make him a bad writer, but it would have guaranteed him a poor mark, possibly a fail, in his exams in our schools.

I have been justifiably scathing about the near-obsession that many English teachers have with spelling mistakes. Their absolute love of that vengeful red pen. However, I could not be indifferent to the psychological damage caused to individuals both in school and in life by their consciousness of being poor spellers. It is the metaphorical equivalent of having a bad stutter or some similar impediment. For this reason, if no other, it is clear that, rather than merely rubbing their noses in it which is all too often the modern practice, the underlying problem must be addressed at secondary school before it is too late and before the problems become entrenched.

To this end I devised an ingeniously simple system for first identifying and then correcting the individual problems of each student. This began with the student specifying, through their own very basic and easily managed research using previously marked scripts, those words or parts of words that were causing them most difficulty, such as the notoriously troublesome 'ie/ei' cluster. Then, knowing where the problems lie, they are able to correct them methodically starting with the most frequent and pernicious and working their way down. As I used to say to teachers when I was describing this system, "If you find in a pupil's work that he or she is regularly making mistakes with a particular component or cluster in certain words that they use a lot, then you have to deal with this as a priority. However, if some pupil tried once, and failed, to correctly spell an unusual word like 'diarrhoea', who gives a shit! They just look it up in the dictionary, like we all do."

The system I invented, following exhaustive research, was truly groundbreaking. I discovered, startlingly, that the raw number of root words involving each verbal and/or consonant cluster in a typical high-school-level dictionary was of the order of only thirty or less with a mere two or three exceptions in each case! The pertinent parts of these lists could be mastered in a very short time, if not actually memorised, by the individual pupil concerned. The system was later published as a very successful textbook. But that is a story for another day.

Getting back to my quarrels with the Establishment that I was telling you about earlier. Because of my strenuous opposition to the increasing bureaucratisation of the education system, I was judged rebellious by the authorities and more and more a threat to their plans.

It is true that, along with my principled objection to the direction in which they were going, I also had, I freely admit it, a huge personal contempt for all bureaucrats. And I didn't mind letting it show.

When I looked around at my superiors in the upper echelons of the education department I was struck by how dull and unimaginative they were as a bunch and I greatly wondered at it. Someone must have chosen them in an interview for these elevated positions. And yet, how could anyone in the full possession of their senses have chosen such arid and lifeless specimens for positions of power and influence? The unanimity of their insignificance was puzzling.

Then, one day, it came to me in a flash as I was watching a nature programme on TV about baboons.

They were chosen, not despite their aridity, but because of it!

As I watched those baboons shamelessly flashing their backsides as they moved swiftly through the trees, I was struck by how ugly and unprepossessing were their preposterously pink posteriors. And yet the baboon's arse is not at all unappealing to an appropriate other baboon, but is, instead, an object of wonder and delight.

Thus was born what I came to call the 'Baboon's ass syndrome' of middle management selection, my version of the common phrase, 'it takes one to know one'. And by no means did I keep it to myself!

You can see why a parting of the ways was not only necessary but entirely mutual.

It all came to a head when the Scottish Education Department decided to revamp post-fifteen education by the introduction of a new system of organisation, called the Standard Grade.

I took a serious and principled objection to the new set-up, mainly on account of its assessment procedures which were highly regressive and formal. They perpetuated the worst excesses of a tightly controlled and highly ritualised form of assessment, to which I have already alluded, but raised it to a higher level of strictness and widened it to include all pupils, including the less academically inclined, for whom it was not only culturally inappropriate but foreseeably problematic. It seemed to me that this further bureaucratisation of the education system would have the effect of limiting free thought and expression by forcing all pupils through the same narrow defile, like cattle being jostled indiscriminately to the slaughterhouse.

Since the proposal was still officially in what was called the Consultative Phase, I felt it necessary to do all in my power to prevent it from being implemented.

Being at the time the Advisor in English for the Lothian region, which included Edinburgh, I organised conferences of the English teachers in my region. I wrote articles for the educational press at a national and subject level and spoke widely at various national conferences and events outlining my objections to this flawed and potentially damaging development.

I took my case to meetings of my fellow advisors in the other parts of Scotland. Many of them found my arguments persuasive enough but were reluctant to support me publicly for fear of the very powerful Her Majesty's Educational Police Force, the Inspectorate, who were propelling the initiative and who governed everything in Scottish education.

I had no such fear, indeed a too-much zest for the confrontation, and sought every opportunity to belittle and deride the individual inspectors with whom I came in contact. This tactic of mine was similar to the morally questionable, but highly effective, tactic of some members of the French officer class, all expert duellists, who in chagrin at their defeat at Waterloo took to going about provoking challenges from their bumbling English counterparts so that they could kill them in the ensuing duel without fear of retribution.

Of course, this did not, in some magical way, retrospectively change the outcome of the battle of Waterloo but it made the officers concerned feel a good deal better about themselves. This pretty much sums up my own situation. In my running conflicts with the Inspectorate I was winning a lot of personal battles, but the war was already lost.

The individual English teachers of my region, Lothian, were enthusiastically supportive of my opposition to the Standard Grade. I remember one particular meeting I organised in one of our secondary schools. After I had made, yet again, a very impassioned speech about the terrible flaws in the Standard Grade, the audience of English teachers was moved to respond very enthusiastically to my call to arms. At the conclusion of the meeting, as I stood alone on the stage, they came rushing up to me expressing hearty support and throwing at my feet hastily scrawled notes containing strongly worded messages of critical dissent that they wished me to pass on to the Scottish Education Department. For a dizzying moment I felt like a latter-day Joan of Arc as their supportive notes piled up like a pyre at my feet. Prophetic, or what?

Mind you, I was not entirely carried away by this extraordinary gesture of support. I knew human nature too well for that. I was perfectly aware that at the first set of traffic lights on their way home in the car these normally timid people would be saying, "What a card Pat is! He sure knows how to put it to those people." By the second set of traffic lights, with reality setting in, they would be saying things like, "Pat does take things a bit too far at times, though, doesn't he?" By the third set of traffic lights it would have become, "Pat who?"

As I have already said, all this took place during what was supposed to be a consultative period. You would have thought that all opinions on this important innovation, even critical ones, would have been welcomed. After all, isn't that the definition of the word 'consult'?

Not so in this case.

The head of Her Majesty's Inspectorate wrote to my director of education in Lothian complaining, in the strongest terms, about my strenuous and very public opposition to their plans and, in particular, about my malign influence on the English teachers of my region (who were, they claimed, not coincidentally, the only group of teachers in the whole of Scotland who actively opposed their plans). They demanded that the education authority should take steps to curb my activities in some way, and at once.

Since there was no love lost between myself and the senior management of the Regional Education Department, it did not exactly break the director's heart to summon me to a peremptory disciplinary hearing to answer the charge against me. He told me about the Letter of Complaint that he had received from Her Majesty's Chief Inspector and their fury that I was foiling, or attempting to foil, their, already well-developed, plans to introduce this initiative in all schools.

You may be sure I had plenty to say in my own defence and I said it forcefully. Logic was the only weapon available to me and I wielded it with skill and incisiveness. It was all to no avail.

Unable to counteract the logic of my position, they were reduced to the expedient of repeating, like a mantra, "We are committed to giving our total support in this, as in all other matters, to the Scottish Education Department and that is what we will do."

When the kangaroo court ended, I was found guilty on all charges and ordered, on pain of dismissal, to desist from writing anything in the national or local press critical of the Standard Grade. On the same terms I was forbidden to even speak publicly on the subject at any event outside of our region of Lothian. They could not very well stop me from speaking to my own English teachers within the region, for that was, after all, my job. More broadly, I was effectively silenced in a way that would have impressed a soviet regime. In fact, one assistant director, hearing of it, said to me (in private, it must be said) that this assault on my freedom of speech was an abomination. After all, as he said, "We are not Czechoslovakia."

The situation could not go on. Eventually my superiors at regional level, because I was strongly supported by my union, agreed to give me early retirement on terms that were very satisfactory to me. At the same time, with me out of the way, the Standard Grade was rolled out all over Scotland.

Much later, when it was safe to do so, because the innovation was firmly and permanently established, many important figures in Scottish education expressed their own misgivings about the development. These voices included, startlingly, my own former boss, the Chief Advisor of Lothian, who wrote an article in *The Times Educational Supplement* denouncing those very aspects of the innovation for which I had been silenced and effectively removed from my post. Yet, he had been an active member of the lynching party that day in the director's office when they gave me the ultimatum, "Shut up or ship out!"

TWO

My professional trajectory had taken me from teacher of English to principal teacher and then to become advisor in English in the large region that included the capital city of Scotland, Edinburgh.

Having started teaching in my home town of Dumbarton in the west of Scotland, in St Patrick's High School which I had attended as a pupil, I taught successively in Canada and in schools in Edinburgh, as well as, latterly, some periods as a simple classroom teacher in the region of Fife, or the Kingdom of Fife, as it is popularly known.

My career could have been described as stellar. From the outset, my abilities as a teacher had been recognised by the school management and by my colleagues and, I am glad to say, by my pupils who never made life difficult for me and, even, seemed on the whole to like me.

This was most marked and most welcome to me amongst the boisterous groups of less academically inclined pupils for whom I always had a great affinity and natural sympathy. They were, after all, largely from the lower socio-economic groups and I came from the same stock as they did.

I was born and grew up in a poor Irish-Catholic enclave in the west of Scotland. Poverty and violence were endemic. The street where I lived had been chosen by the original Irish immigrants because it was easy to defend in the days of the vicious anti-Irish pogroms that were part of daily life at that time. Just barricade each end of the street and the fighting men in the middle would take care of the rest.

There was, understandably, a great camaraderie amongst the inhabitants of the Vennel, as our street was called locally, and I could not have been more proud of the community into which I was born.

I said there was great poverty and violence. There was. But, for the most part, it was mitigated.

The poverty by the fact that everyone was poor, so it was not felt so keenly. This is well exemplified in the almost universal dearth of shoes among the younger population. It was normal to go barefoot in the summer months. In all other conditions of weather the poverty-labelling wellington boots were ubiquitously worn. When you're all wearing wellies, and getting the same circular whip-burn at the top of your calves from time to time, who cares? This was the Vennel, not some fashion catwalk in Paris or Milan. And none the worse for that, if you ask me.

As for the violence, it was characterised mostly by what was called the 'square go'. A square go was a man-on-man scrap which involved no use of weapons and, absolutely, no involvement of a third party.

I vividly remember one particular square go. I was about ten at the time and had just been at the pictures, as we called it. As I exited the cinema, I came upon what was obviously a fight at the entrance to an offshoot of the Vennel, called Kane's Pend, which was populated, almost exclusively, by people from the far west of Ireland.

As you can imagine, flushed with my celluloid dreams, I was enormously excited at the prospect of this spectacle and pressed closer to get a better view. I soon found myself in the front rank of the circle of spectators. Easy for the small boy that I was.

The scene that met my astonished gaze was extraordinarily exciting.

In the centre of the circle was a well-known hardman by the name of Heudie Elliot. His shirt was bloodied and torn half to shreds. Around him I could discern a number of supine bodies. It transpired that these were brothers. A quarrel had developed between Heudie and the youngest brother that led to the first square go. When Heudie had vanquished this one, each of his brothers in ascending order of age took his place and suffered the same fate. These were the strict rules of engagement for such affairs.

By the time I arrived Heudie was holding the oldest brother up by the neck about to deliver the *coup de grâce*. The old grandmother of the boys, a corpse-gaunt virago called Hannah O'Donnell, was capering about and hurling imprecations in Irish on the head of the redoubtable Heudie.

I have seldom seen such a heroic figure as at that moment Heudie presented to my eyes as he majestically threw his head back and shouted out to the night air and the assembled crowd those words that would forever resound in my memory: "I know," said he, "that St Patrick, by the grace of God, banished the snakes from Ireland, but why, in the name of God tell me, why did he have to dump the whole lot o' yous in Kane's Pend?"

With that, he delivered the final crushing blow and thus fell – but only for now – the last of the O'Donnells.

Much later, I witnessed an incident involving the same Heudie but with an entirely different outcome.

Our tenement looked on to the 'back' or 'green' of an adjoining tenement. This courtyard may have started out as a lawn, but it was no longer green, for whatever grass there once was had been scuffed away long since, leaving only black, hard earth.

Every Friday night the neighbours of this tenement used to congregate after the pubs shut to drink, sing songs and tell stories. There was an accordion player and Tommy Toole who played an improbable double-bass.

My two brothers and I would sneak out of bed to watch, entranced, this engrossing spectacle. To the cry of "Give us your pleasure", one after another of the group would step forward to sing the song that was affectionately and firmly associated with them. Nutty McDermott would sing 'When They Begin the Beguine'. Dinnie Mulhearn would regale the company with a sweet rendition of his favourite, 'Eileen Ogh'. For hours on end popular songs and Irish songs would succeed each other with barely a pause. It was intoxicating stuff for the wee boy that I was and I eagerly soaked up every bead and bubble of the experience before it could evaporate forever.

Nor, being Irish, were prose and poetry neglected. During the intermissions in the music someone would be sure to recite something from Yeats or John Clarence Mangan, say, 'The Isle of Innisfree' or the very patriotic 'My dark Rosaleen'. Dinny McGrory would invariably entertain the company with his version of the classic monologue by Robert Service, called 'Dangerous Dan McGrew', which was a great favourite of the crowd. And if Dinny forgot the words from time to time, through drink taken, there was no end of people who were able to prompt him back on track. Sean McManus would inspire everyone with his spirited declamation of Robert Emmet's famously noble 'Speech from the Dock' on the occasion of his being sentenced to death for treason against the British Crown which concludes with those stirring words, 'Let not my epitaph be written till Ireland has taken its place among the nations of the earth. Then, and not until then, let my epitaph be written'. And, for the record, it wasn't, and then it was.

But to get back to Heudie.

One evening, my brothers and I became aware, just out of our sight at first, of a serious fight which had broken out in the vicinity of the entertainment. The singing stopped at once and all eyes turned in the direction of the incident. The fight between the two combatants soon took them out into the centre of the green and my brothers and I became privileged spectators of the unfolding drama.

A long-simmering resentment between Heudie and a certain Wattie Glover had eventually spilled out into open warfare.

It was a mismatch if ever you saw one. Wattie Glover had a head and twenty pounds on Heudie. Furthermore, he was a promising amateur heavyweight boxer. Heudie was a very good scrapper but lacked any professional training and had more than a bit of a beer belly on him. Nonetheless, he was game and was giving pretty much as good as he was getting.

For a time at least!

Then the odds began to weigh in Wattie's favour and he began putting Heudie down with crushing blows. Each time Heudie would get up straight away and lumber forward for more. Wattie Glover kept saying, "Stay down, Elliot!" But it did no good. To the cry of "Fuck you!", Heudie kept coming back at him. It was the most courageous thing I ever saw and my heart went out entirely to the indomitable Heudie.

Eventually, after one last telling put-down the crowd surged forward, silently, as one and compassionately engulfed both fighters and drew them both back to the party zone. The music started again as if nothing had happened and more spiritedly than before. Later, Heudie even 'gave us his pleasure' which was 'Phil the Fluter's Ball' and Wattie joined him in the chorus.

Thus ended another typical Friday night in the Vennel.

However, Friday night was merely the vigil of the feast that was Saturday morning in the Vennel.

I will turn my attention to that but only after I have recounted the story of the greatest square-go in the history of the Vennel.

THREE

The greatest square go in the history of the Vennel was not at all a square go of the traditional kind.

Normally square goes develop spontaneously as a result of some mutual antagonism or supposed slight. Tempers flare and the resort to violence ensues. This square go was different in that it did not arise out of any personal animosity and, far from being a hot-blooded response to some indignity or other, it was planned and set up meticulously and cold-bloodedly in advance. It was more or less a boxing match to settle the honours between our community of the Vennel and a tough, rival Irish Catholic community on the outskirts of town. My own father was the chosen champion of the Vennel and a fellow called Nicky Connolly was the champion of Brucehill.

The venue, it was decided, would be the premises of The Ancient Order of Hibernians, otherwise known as the Hibs Hall. This venue was selected for obvious reasons but particularly in order that the fight would be out of the sight of the local constabulary who took particular exception at that time to people fighting in public and would have put a stop to it before it could even begin.

It is a great tribute to the people of both communities that the police never got wind of this planned fight despite it being the main topic of conversation in both these communities for weeks prior to it taking place.

As it turned out, the event did not lack for spectators for, although no one but the combatants and their chosen seconds (to ensure fair play) were allowed into the hall, some people clambered up onto the high windows that ringed the hall to watch the proceedings, perched perilously on the very narrow window-ledges and clinging precariously to the thin wire netting that covered the windows. It was a dangerous and, at best, uncomfortable way of seeing into the hall and would have been available only to a few intrepid souls. Nevertheless, such was the mythic fame of the contest that those who subsequently claimed to have personally witnessed the fight could be counted in their thousands.

On the day arranged, the two combatants, my father and Nicky Connolly, accompanied by their respective seconds, John McAllister and Cowlar Whallen, entered the hall. They then, in a very Irish way, ceremoniously locked the door behind them and threw the key along the floor of the hall to be retrieved by the 'best man' or winner. He would then use it to open the door and walk through it triumphantly at the conclusion of the contest.

The fight itself was an epic one and went on for a very long time (some said the whole day but this is wildly improbable). At any rate in the popular imagination the battle between the two combatants became magnified out of all proportion and grew to rival the famous big fight between John Wayne and Victor McLaglen in that much-loved film, *The Quiet Man*.

Like in that great film, nobody is quite sure of the actual outcome due to the highly restricted visibility of the spectators and the long time that elapsed before the two exhausted combatants and their appropriate seconds exited the hall en masse. The Brucehill legends have it that Nicky Connolly won but in the legends of the Vennel it was my father that proved victorious. Either way it was impossible for anyone to be entirely sure.

I personally have no doubt that my father won: purely and simply because he never said he did! If he had been defeated he would have confessed it readily enough to us, because of his own personal code of honour but also out of respect for Nicky Connolly whom he acknowledged as a very redoubtable opponent and with whom he had subsequently a close friendship that lasted all their lives. I have no doubt that Nicky maintained his own personal omerta on the event for much the same reasons as my father.

The day following the fight, while my father was working in a ditch by the side of the town bridge, Police Sergeant Archie Findlay accompanied by a young constable turned up and ordered my father out of the ditch for questioning.

"You were fighting last night, McLaughlin," said the sergeant.

"No' me," replied my father.

"Man, look at the state of your face, of course you were fighting last night," persisted the sergeant.

"These marks? That's down to my wife, Mary. You know her and you know what a vicious woman she can be when I come home the worse of the wear wi' the drink."

"Nonsense, McLaughlin. You might as well come clean, we know all about it. We have just this minute left Nicky Connolly's bedside at the Cottage Hospital where they are treating him for a suspected broken jaw."

"And did Nicky say that I did it?" asked my father innocently.

"No, of course he did not, for everybody knows that you Papists would never gie each other up, especially no' tae the polis," replied the disgruntled sergeant. "But mark my words, and mark them well, I intend to get to the bottom of this affair, no matter how long it takes!"

One little part of me wishes that he had carried out his promise, for if he had, we might have got a final answer to that most perplexing question – who actually won?

As if it mattered.

My father wasn't a huge man but he had the physique of a middleweight boxer. He was compact, muscular and immensely strong. His favourite game at home was getting one of us children or a visiting neighbour to sit on one of our kitchen chairs. Then, using only one hand clasped round one of the back legs of the chair he would lift chair and occupant three feet in the air, apparently effortlessly. This feat required exceptional power in the wrist, arm and shoulder as well as considerable juggling skill to align perfectly, and then maintain, the balance of both seat and sitter. If you don't think that this is all that impressive, why don't you try it yourself – using just an empty chair! See how you get on with that!

My father's other great trick when he was in a good mood was walking on his hands, something that required great acrobatic skill.

It was quite a sight to see him, using the palms of his hands as feet and with his legs pointing impeccably skywards, manoeuvring his way, tentatively but impeccably, round the table in the middle of our cramped little kitchen. My father was a veritable one-man circus all to ourselves.

Talking about circuses reminds me of an amusing incident concerning my father, or more accurately, my mother, which has a strong circus connection.

My father was the all-too-willing victim of the male pub culture that was prevalent at the time and, so, never found the time, by his way of it, to take my mother out in a social way. The only occasion that I can ever remember my father taking my mother out on what you could term a date was when he took her to a showing at the local cinema of the film, *The Quiet Man*, which was, for understandable reasons, a particular favourite of the men of the area. Fortunately, my mother enjoyed it very much herself on account of its Irishness and its outstanding comedy.

This apparent lack of any romantic propensity on the part of my father rankled greatly with my mother who sought every opportunity to berate him for his negligence in this regard. The day the circus came to our town, which happened every two years or so, provided her with a heaven-sent opportunity to apply further pressure on my father.

The appearance in our town of Cotter's Circus was a very big occasion for everyone, at all levels in our population. Though it had obviously been programmed and prepared for much in advance by the parties concerned, for some reason it always came to us in the Vennel as a tremendous surprise, like a sudden clap of unexpected thunder.

In us children it induced an excitement amounting almost to delirium. We ogled with awe the large number of huge and heavily laden waggons that lumbered onto the Town Common containing the enormous pieces of heavy equipment that were needed for the setting up of the circus tent and the fairground that would be created round it.

The fairground, when it materialised, would contain several large engines of entertainment, such as the fast Moon Rocket (my personal favourite) and the massive, swinging Bostons (called Bo'suns in the local dialect). These great swaying behemoths were always popular with us kids for they never failed to produce a cascading bonanza of coins of every description that fell out of the pockets of the male clients of these monsters as they lost their hold and slid down the steeply sloping floors of the great baskets.

There was always the mandatory Ghost Train which was a magnet, especially to the young men and girls, for it never failed to produce delicious shudders of fear and horror as it trundled its unlit way through galleries that depicted scenes of horrific violence and ghastly supernatural visions. Some of the most terrible and frightening of these had the happy effect of forcing many a young girl, consumed by fear, to throw herself into the arms of the salivating satyr that had fiendishly and surreptitiously taken the place of her erstwhile shy and awkward boyfriend.

Then there was the plethora of smaller scale entertainments, like the shooting galleries, the coconut shies and the roll-a-penny games of chance that produced armfuls of prizes in the form of balloons and cuddly toys to the delight of both parents and children.

However, undoubtedly the greatest spectacle of all, which never failed to draw a huge crowd was the opening parade of the circus.

This began with the elephants pulling along the highly colourful and heavily reinforced carriages containing caged lions, tigers, a bear or two, sea lions and several chimpanzees. These were followed by a procession of the human personnel of the circus, the ringmaster, clowns, jugglers, stilt-walkers, tightrope performers and a great sufficiency of very shapely and short-skirted trapeze artistes to keep well entertained the male portion of the watchers.

Warm applause always accompanied the strutting and mustachioed little ball of muscles that was the circus strongman whose trademark barbell seemed to float on his massive shoulders as if it was a thing of nothing. (Perhaps it was.)

Taking up the rear of the parade was a troop of beautiful and highly spirited horses with riders in the saddle who were dressed in full cowboy gear and who waved their broad-brimmed hats constantly and jauntily in all directions.

For me, personally, it was a particular thrill to watch the handlers putting up the big top. A veritable army of roustabouts, as they are called, would swoop down on the piles of waiting equipment, like ants issuing en masse from the nest, and proceed speedily to turn these disparate pieces of wood, ironmongery and canvas into a magnificent and capacious tent. Watching their seemingly frantic but actually very adroit and skilled activity, was like watching a film that is being very fast-forwarded.

Then appeared in all its glory the big top, fluttering with flags and pennants and surrounded by its satellite fairground that blazed with colour and swiftly-changing lights and was thronged with eager, happy people bent on enjoyment and the innocent desire to be entertained.

Surely, must have thought my mother, surely all of this could not fail to touch the heart, even of an anti-romantic like my father. Without too much ceremony, after outlining the importance of the occasion and the wonderful delights it promised, then she played her ace card and said, "Pat, if you were half a man at all, you would take me to the circus."

My father instantly replied, not without a certain cockiness, "Don't be ridiculous, Mary, if I was half a man I would be in the bloody circus."

Back to the drawing board, Mary.

FOUR

Saturday morning was the season of great plenty for the residents of the Vennel. For the only time in the week, there was money about, because of the men's wages, and everyone was happy.

The Vennel became a veritable piazza. The street was filled with happy children at play: the boys, as usual, aimlessly kicking a ball about; the more imaginative girls singing jolly and complicated songs while cawing ropes or playing peever and other of their ingenious street games. The women were cheerily going from shop to shop in an ecstasy of purchasing. The men were either in the pub or congregating in Alex Murphy's barber shop to talk about Celtic's next game or about boxing, their second great passion.

Ah, Murphy's Barber Shop! I used to love going to that bastion of male privilege. The walls were festooned with photographs and posters of all the great, mainly Irish, boxers of the past, like John L Sullivan, Gentleman Jim Corbett, Jim (Cinderella Man) Braddock, Jack Dempsey and the greatly loved Mickey Walker. There were also some action photos of our most famous local boxer, 'Sweet' Teddy O'Neill, whose family emigrated to the United States from the Vennel some years before. Teddy became a Golden Gloves winner at Madison Square Garden and his career was avidly followed.

The bustle in the street was not limited to people of all ages. It was amplified by the army of street traders that invaded our neighbourhood at that time. There were handcarts selling fruit and vegetables. Others selling books and knick-knacks. Then there was the pedal-powered ice-cream cart of Signor Casci which so delighted the children with its traditional vertical stripes of chocolate and cream and its alluring Neapolitan jingle.

The very popular strolling street-singers always put in an appearance in the backyards of the Vennel at this comparatively lucrative time.

The more well-doing of these troubadours usually availed themselves of the services of a cute little monkey that had great novelty value and helped enormously in the collection of donations by climbing up the slim drainpipes of the tall tenements and holding out a sweet little begging paw to the would-be donors.

These street-singers were never local and were part of an army of such entertainers that travelled about the country, in a professionally criss-cross manner, from locality to locality.

In the religiously divided world of the west of Scotland it paid (literally and metaphorically) to take careful account of your audience. Choosing the wrong song could be a disaster, if not something really worse. However, these were highly experienced people and knew what they were doing.

I remember one day when I was walking down the Vennel with my Uncle Tommy in the direction of the Cross which was the spot where the Vennel intersected the main road from Glasgow. As we neared the Cross a very smartly dressed and dapper man jumped off the back of a slow-moving bus and started walking up the Vennel, almost as if he was in a hurry to get some place. As he passed my Uncle Tommy and me, he cheerily cried out, "Hey, pal, this is a Catholic area, isn't it?" My Uncle Tommy replied, "Aye, mate, wall to wall." Without breaking his stride, the man, who turned out to be a professional street-singer, began singing at the top of his impressive voice, 'Hail, Queen of Heaven'. This was a well-known hymn to Mary, the Mother of God, that still is very popular all over the English-speaking Catholic world. You could call these street-singers many things, but daft is not one of them.

Paddy Conroy, the coalman, never failed to put in an appearance at this time with his horse and cart. It was a good day to deliver coal to the people because the chance of getting paid up front was much greater. For us kids, Paddy and his horse were a very welcome addition to the street scene. The horse was often parked for what seemed like hours in front of MacIlhaw's pub and so we could get a really long, fascinated look at it. It was virtually the only contact with wildlife that we had and we treasured those moments.

Paddy's horse, called Trojan (was Paddy a covert classicist?), may have been his owner's unwitting accomplice in his moments of dissipation in MacIlhaw's bar, but he was, nonetheless, legendary for his holiness. It was said that Trojan genuflected, or in his case, went down on one hoof, when he passed the chapel. Chapel is the word in general use in the west of Scotland for a Catholic church to distinguish it from those Protestant. I, myself, never witnessed this act of reverence on Trojan's part, but I have no reason to doubt it, based on the large number of people of unimpeachable character who claim to have seen Trojan, in this remarkable way, pay his respect to the presence of the Blessed Sacrament in the chapel.

Just opposite MacIlhaw's bar there was the pawnshop owned by Mr Laidlaw. Lum Hat Laidlaw, as he was called, was a man of indeterminate age with slicked-down hair who sported very high collars and was the perfect picture of a Dickensian chief clerk. He had acquired his nickname of Lum Hat from the fact that he constantly wore a hat with a very high crown perched on his head like a chimney (the local dialect word for 'chimney' is 'lum'). For all his somewhat comic appearance, he was a very powerful person in the life of the Vennel and central, in a way, to its orderly functioning.

Every Saturday morning, without fail, Lum Hat's pawnshop would be thronged with people redeeming their coats, shoes, suits and frocks which had been pawned the week before. These items of clothing would be taken home and proudly worn during the relaxing hours of the weekend and, especially, at Sunday Mass.

On Monday morning these same items of clothing would be faithfully returned to the pawnshop where they would earn just enough to supplement the dwindling family finances at the start of the ensuing week.

It was a very good system for all the parties concerned. Mr Laidlaw had a business he could rely on and the people of the area had moth-free, clean storage for their best clothes, as well as a small, but significant, addition to their finances when they were at their most diluted.

One local wag, called Hawk Adams, put a pair of shoes into the pawn so regularly that it was not worth Lum Hat's trouble to unwrap them and examine them every time. Consequently, each week Hawk would hand over his shoes already packaged. The money would be exchanged and Hawk's package would sit, untouched, on the shelf till he redeemed it the following week.

Eventually, Hawk took to wrapping up in the parcel, not his shoes, but a half brick of approximately the same weight. This gave him the use of his shoes for the whole week at the net cost of only the slight interest on redemption.

I don't know if Lum Hat ever suspected he was being duped in this way. Knowing him, as unfortunately I did, I rather doubt if he would be taken in by such an obvious ploy. However, even if he was, he would have had no incentive to disrupt a perfectly satisfactory piece of business which suited both parties and harmed neither.

I always hated the few occasions that I was forced to go to the pawnshop. I found the experience deeply shameful and embarrassing. This feeling of shame that I experienced was entirely ridiculous for there is nothing inherently shameful in using your possessions as security for a loan.

The rich do it all the time and they are applauded and even honoured for it. This oversensitivity was a flaw in my character which I realised only with maturity was the result of deep social insecurity and feelings of inadequacy.

My younger brother, Eddie, by contrast, bounded up and down the stairs to the pawn as lightsome as a deer. How I envied him his hearty ingenuousness and simple, carefree spirit.

Nothing that happened to me in later life could ever dim those happy days of my Vennel childhood.

Of course, like anywhere else, the Vennel had its darker moments, even on a Saturday. It was one Saturday morning that my wee pal, Charlie Hannaway, and I discovered the dead body of Chesty McGuigan.

With no school to go to at the weekend, bored and in search of adventure, we had decided to explore the forbidden precincts of McGowan's Tower, a derelict building just off the Vennel.

This former tenement or multi-storey warehouse had fallen into disrepair long since and been abandoned. In the course of its deterioration all the internal floors of the building had collapsed leaving only a series of narrow ledges that ran round the structure and reached up to the roof. The whole scene had a frightening and chilling look with scraps of lath and plaster hanging horridly from the ledges in the spectral gloom of the cavernous interior.

Naturally, the structure had been condemned long since as unsafe and kept locked and boarded up on the orders of the council.

Surmounting these security precautions presented no great difficulty for the pair of inquisitive nine-year-olds that we were at the time. It was not long after we had got inside and had adjusted our eyes to the darkness that we saw the dead body of Chesty, a well-known local alcoholic, lying amidst the bricks and rubble.

We were filled with alarm, fear and revulsion. It was obvious, even to us, that poor Chesty was dead and yet, apart from a small pool of blood under his head and some odd angulation of his arms and legs, he looked remarkably serene.

We knew that Chesty and his fellow alkies were in the habit of using one of the more ample ledges higher up the building as sleeping quarters. We instinctively looked up, for we felt sure that he had fallen from that ledge. The only question was: had he rolled over in a drunken stupor or had he been pushed, perhaps inadvertently, in the course of a scuffle? Ominously, it was clear to us that the ledge in question was empty. Had his friends taken off – and, if so, why?

Charlie and I became greatly alarmed at what we found ourselves involved in and, curiously, began to feel guilty as if our discovery of the tragedy made us, somehow, complicit in the event. This feeling of guilt was exacerbated by our consciousness that we were only in this predicament because we had done a bad and forbidden thing in going into McGowan's Tower in the first place. You may be sure that we exited that building, fled the scene, as it were, at top speed.

We were too frightened to tell our parents of our discovery because that would have brought its own retribution. It never crossed our minds to go to the police (that would have been unthinkable in our community). But we had to tell someone!

Being, as we were, deeply troubled that we had made the discovery in the act of doing something that was very wrong and, perhaps, sinful, we decided to go to confession and tell the priest. Confession for the youth of the parish was regularly available on a Saturday morning in our parish.

I don't remember anything about the actual confession itself. To the scrupulous and guilt-wracked child that I was, only the absolution mattered. The confession itself went past in a blur of determination to get it all off my chest and to frankly and faithfully confess my imagined sin.

Strangely, my memory of the whole event ends there. I remember nothing else about the incident or its aftermath. Presumably the priest would have contacted the police (he could have done this easily without breaching the seal of confession). Presumably there would have been a follow-up investigation and a burial. I know nothing of this at all.

It is not so surprising that the subsequent developments escaped my notice, because it was a key part of the protective code of our community that children should be strictly guarded from any contact with things that are unedifying or shameful. This communal delicacy towards the young is somewhat analogous to the manner in which the sea in its compassion lovingly enfolds and seals off the sinking body of some poor drowned sailor.

FIVE

In the latter stages of my advisory career I had, bit by bit, adapted to myself a supplementary career as a heavy drinker. It was a career in which I greatly flourished and in which I had an extremely high profile.

This is how I first got to know the people who appointed me to the new job I was about to take up before my heart attack. They were prominent councillors in the Labour-dominated local government of the city of Edinburgh and represented wards in Craigmillar, a vast estate of working-class rehousing that had many social problems. It was considered at that time to be the drugs capital of Europe.

The councillors and I became great friends and enthusiastic members of an enlarged social circle dominated by politics, football (they were avid Hibs fans and I was a lifelong and passionate Celtic supporter, so compatible) and a great mutual lust for fun and jocularity.

They were well aware of my strengths as well as my failings. When I gave up the drink some two years before, it did not go unnoticed in the hostelries for which

Edinburgh is famous and gave me a certain kind of astonished celebrity among the heavy drinkers of that city. Subsequently, some people I knew came up to me and told to my face that they had also given up the drink, basically because they thought, "If Pat could do it, so could anyone".

The journey from socially-acceptable drinking to alcoholism is a slow process. The decline is almost imperceptible at first, but inexorable for the addicted. In the early stages of my progress down this slippery slope my drinking did not seem to be a problem. Indeed, quite the opposite. It was, if anything, a social asset. Recounting all the hilarious episodes of drink-induced boldness I used to engage in, gave great amusement to my friends and colleagues and made me a popular presence at all our social gatherings.

Things got a bit more serious as my drinking proceeded apace and began to affect my performance at work. I was protected for a time from the consequences of my misconduct by a combination of native wit and cunning and outrageous luck.

The wit and cunning came to my aid on those occasions when I was facing situations at work where, due to their high profile and the public scrutiny that went with it, I could not afford to be anything but completely sober. In cases like this I just seemed to be able to 'screw the bobbin', as they say, or, in other words, behave myself by steering clear of the drink.

Whenever this career-preserving sixth sense failed, all I had to rely on was luck and, fortunately, that came to my aid on many occasions, such as the one I am about to relate to you.

Briefly, at the time, in addition to my regular work with the local education department, I was working as a part-time visiting lecturer in the extramural department of the arts faculty of Edinburgh University. I was providing a course on the modern novel to an evening-class group made up of members of the public as well as students and (some) staff from other faculties in the university who were wishing to expand their horizons.

Things had gone well for the first four or five nights of the course. Then it all went horribly wrong.

It was my habit to go to Murphy's bar in the centre of Edinburgh to put the finishing touches to my upcoming lecture over a toastie and a glass of beer. On this occasion, whether I had arrived at Murphy's with more drink in me than I thought or took one too many with my toastie I cannot say, but I found myself a little woozy. When I stood up to go, I stumbled, just a little, but it was enough for the sharp-eyed barmaid who witnessed it to say, "You've had a fair whack the night, Paddy. Do you want a coffee to sober you up?"

I declined her offer and said, "I'm fine. I just need to clear my head. The fresh air will put me right."

Now anyone with the slightest experience of drink will tell you that fresh air only makes things worse. By the time I reached the university I was well and truly drunk and dreaded the walk down the steeply raked steps of the lecture hall to the dais at the front. Somehow I managed it and gratefully grasped the lectern which alone kept me from falling down.

I looked up. What I saw was not the usual class but a horribly distorted and melting sea of faces, like a TV screen that has gone crazy. I was obviously in no state to give anything remotely resembling a lecture, so I said, "Tonight we are going to do something different for a change. It's called reading round the room. You start."

I pointed at a young man sitting at the extreme left at the back of the room. He started reading from the beginning of *Sons and Lovers* by D H Lawrence which was our projected text for that evening. Strangely enough, the others in the class followed him faithfully, and apparently contentedly, in sequence, each reading a page or so of the book. Somehow we got through the hour and the class left at the end of the session as if nothing had happened. No one seemed to take offence at my bizarre behaviour. No one, subsequently, complained to the university about my being drunk in class.

I could not believe that I had escaped, apparently unscathed, and was naturally very grateful for it, but I was mystified nonetheless and was in a terrible state of apprehension, shame and embarrassment when I turned up the following week. I needn't have worried: the class was all there and the lecture proceeded in the normal way to its conclusion.

After the lecture I couldn't help reiterating my apologies to an elderly class member who was a retired professor in the chemistry department. She said to me, "Don't worry. We all know what happened last week. You know, your little slip. Nobody took it the wrong way. In fact it was quite funny and gave us a good laugh afterwards. I think that everyone liked getting the chance to read out loud in class. It brought back memories of happy schooldays. Anyway, most of them are a bunch of show-offs and couldn't wait to hear the sound of their own voice. Forget about it!"

However, though on the surface, by luck and some sharp footwork, everything seemed to be going on fine, I was well aware that underneath the surface the supporting beams of my life were loosening and threatening to collapse the building. Things that had seemed funny before just weren't funny anymore. The consequences were piling up like dirty snow at the side of the road.

When I began to suffer from the dreaded blackouts I knew that I had a serious problem.

To those lucky enough not to be alcoholics, let me explain. An alcoholic blackout means that, though well drunk, you can be functioning apparently normally – and even appear sober as happened to me on many occasions – but the CCTV of your mind is switched off and nothing is being recorded. You later have no memory whatsoever of what happened during the period of blackout.

The really strange thing about this phenomenon is that it is not always a blanket failure of memory, it can be selective in a very odd way. I remember once having a discussion with a pal who referred to a conversation we had had two nights before. I could recall the conversation perfectly well and everyone else who was present at the time, but nothing of him or anything that involved him. It was as if he, alone, had been surgically removed from my memory. There is no reason for this that I can think of, for he was a perfectly nice guy and a good friend of mine.

Of course, blackouts are very worrying things. If someone was having a blackout, for example, and was accused of some crime, they could have no defence to offer.

The great seriousness of blackouts and their consequences hit home to me one night at a meeting of Alcoholics Anonymous.

Across the room from me there was a prosperous-looking man in his middle years. He was strikingly handsome in the manner of Caesar Romero, a matinee idol of the forties and fifties. The plethora of rings and jewellery he exhibited bespoke a possible traveller background.

Anyway, when it came his turn to speak this fellow said, "I had a blackout once (he did not mean 'just once' but 'once upon a time') and came out of it to find myself in a prison cell with another guy. I said to him, 'Where am I?' He replied, 'Saughton Prison.' 'And what the fuck am I doing in Saughton Prison?' I asked him. 'Seven years, pal. For manslaughter,' he replied."

Following the terrible event caused by heavy drinking, he had gone through the subsequent trial, conviction and incarceration with absolutely no memory of any of it.

Blackouts lasting this long are unusual, but not unheard of. So, you can easily understand my concern when I began to experience regular, but, fortunately in my case, short-term blackouts.

The blackouts and other things that were happening in my life made me realise that I needed help.

I wasn't daft, whatever else I was, so I knew that Alcoholics Anonymous was the only way to go. I had a strong, and I concede, unfair contempt for those medical and social agencies that exist to help alcoholics. These people are sincere and well intentioned and can, no doubt, help people with mild drinking problems but they are useless for real alcoholics, mainly because they are so naive. True alcoholics can, and do, run rings round them.

I know this because I had previous experience of trying the medical route. But even then I wasn't fooling myself enough not to know I was choosing the soft option, the polite and easy-going alternative to the real thing. Alcoholics Anonymous is the real thing. AA, I soon discovered, is a tough programme that aims at total abstinence and is composed of hardy people who do not mince their words and are not easily fooled, for as all the world knows 'you can't kid a kidder'.

I had found my way to the doors of AA on a number of previous occasions but they had always ended with me falling off the waggon and going back to the drink. This was because I had not yet reached rock bottom and frankly admitted my total helplessness with regard to alcohol.

Then, in the most ordinary of circumstances, on a day that posed no particular challenges, threats or problems, I had an experience that quite literally changed my life.

I was alone in the house getting ready to go out, inevitably to the pub. For some reason I couldn't find my house keys. I could not go out without them as it was a bitterly cold November day with a mercilessly whipping wind. I was frightened to leave the house on such a day without the prospect of getting back in when I needed to. Irrational fears and terrors of the simplest things in life are the common lot of the confirmed alcoholic.

As I went about the house, searching for the keys in all the most unlikely places as well as the most likely, my panic – and my urgent need for a drink – was mounting by the minute and my search was becoming ever more frantic. At this point, as I started to walk into one of the bedrooms that I had searched multiple times before, I had a very strange experience that I still can't explain all these years later.

I suddenly saw myself in full flesh and blood, not as a ghost or spectre but in complete physical form, coming towards me. As we met at the door this other me stepped slightly aside to let me enter. I walked into the middle of the room and, throwing my arms wide in the air, I called out in a loud voice, really shouted, "Pat, you're an alcoholic!"

Then something happened that I can only describe as miraculous. The room was suddenly suffused in an unearthly radiance and a great sense of joy and exhilaration permeated my whole being. At that moment, as it were, the chains on my wrists fell to the floor and the prison gates opened for me as they did for St Peter in the Acts of the Apostles. I was free!

I walked out of the room and the first thing I saw, there on a table by the door and the first place I had looked, was my set of house keys. How could I have missed them?

I immediately left the house and went straight to a meeting of AA.

AA works because it provides a venue and a platform for alcoholics to meet and share their experiences and to gain comfort and support from other people's stories. However, to be really effective it requires the commitment of its self-volunteering members to a very demanding and rigorous programme of rehabilitation and moral regeneration.

The primary tenet of AA is that alcoholism is an illness whose dimensions are physical, mental or psychological and spiritual. AA puts a great deal of stress on the need for spiritual recovery. This is outlined in what is called the *Big Book* and contains the famous twelve steps to recovery from alcoholism. These famous twelve steps, as I later discovered, are based on the spiritual exercises of St Ignatius of Loyola.

The first, crucial, step is to acknowledge that you are powerless over alcohol and that your life is a total mess because of this. The second step is to acknowledge that only a higher power can restore you to sanity. This concept of the higher power causes much confusion and misunderstanding to people both inside and outside of AA. The higher power you invoke in the second step is not necessarily, though it can be, obviously, a religious power. It is the higher power of 'your understanding' and, as such, could take any form so long as it assists you. I have known atheistic communists in AA and none of them experienced any problems with the second step.

The other steps involve such things as taking a moral inventory of your life and making amends to those you have harmed by your alcoholism, so long as this does not cause harm, offence or embarrassment to them or to anyone else.

These steps are designed, not merely to help the alcoholic to stay off the drink, but to rebuild his or her life in sobriety. Sobriety is a higher and more exalted state than merely abstaining from alcohol. AA doesn't claim to cure your alcoholism, that will remain with you all your life, but it allows you to function as a complete human being with respect for yourself and others. Through honest and humble commitment to the principles of AA, one day at a time, you are enabled, phoenix-like, to rise majestically from the ashes of your former life as a hopeless addict.

The twelfth step in the programme of Alcoholics Anonymous is literally outgoing. This is when, having achieved your own sobriety, again, I stress, one day at a time, you carry the message to other alcoholics and do all you can to assist and support fellow sufferers. This is particularly called for when they are going through a crisis and are having an urgent craving for alcohol and are on the point of succumbing to it. At such a time the good twelve-stepper is worth his or her weight in gold.

My brother, Tommy, was an excellent twelve-stepper. He was kind-hearted and approachable and known to all for his cheerfulness and good humour, as well as for his great AA wisdom and knowledge. Because of this Tommy was often contacted by fellow members of AA when they were in crisis.

By the nature of these emergencies, the need for help often occurs at unsociable hours, sometimes the middle of the night.

No matter the hour, Tommy would go immediately to be by their side and see them through the crisis. Sometimes doing this required him to make round trips of many miles. Since Tommy didn't own a car – or even a bike – he made all of these journeys on foot. By this he had acquired the nickname of 'Walk On Tommy'.

He was still 'walking on' to help fellow addicts right up to his death (of cancer) some years ago. May God have mercy on his wonderfully generous soul.

One day at a time, of course.

SIX

My friends, the councillors, David Brown and Paul Nolan by name, that I told you about earlier, were particularly pleased at my transformation because they had a situation in their constituency in which I could greatly assist them. But only in my capacity as a confirmed ex-drinker.

David and Paul controlled everything in Craigmillar and were so popular that, as the saying has it, their votes in the election were weighed, rather than counted.

As I have already pointed out, Craigmillar had a great many problems, all stemming from poverty and the lack of opportunity and leading to high rates of addiction and, consequently, of criminality. To counteract this, the community itself had set up a community organisation, supported by the local councillors, called the Craigmillar Festival Society, which had sections dealing with housing, employment, social advocacy and, crucially and most provocatively, the arts. All of this substantial and, at times, innovative activity earned the society a high reputation nationally and substantive admiration further afield.

The Craigmillar Festival Society was like a cross between a political party and a mini town council. The members, the community, met regularly in assembly and passed motions democratically that affected the broad governance of the society.

At the same time, it was the first port of call for every type of problem that any large working-class community is bound to have. Its officers came from the people in a way that no ordinary council organisation could match. The Craigmillar Festival Society was robust in defending its community and got in return the love and the trust that it deserved.

One of their existing initiatives was called the Vocational Training Unit (VTU) which was funded jointly by the City of Edinburgh Council and the European Social Fund. It was a scheme designed to get the most problematic long-term unemployed back into work. The manager of the VTU had just left to take up a post elsewhere and there was no one to run the organisation.

The community leaders and the local councillors were loath to abandon the initiative for the benefits it afforded the local community and particularly loath to lose the funding that went with it. So they offered the job to me.

This was the position that I was days from taking up when I suffered my heart attack. To their credit, the leaders of the Festival Society, Jack O'Donnell and Tom Farmer, within days of my attack, came to my hospital bed to assure me that the job would still be there for me, however long my recovery took. This gesture did not at all surprise me, for I knew the temper of those people, but it did make me very happy and relieved, for by this time that job meant the world to me.

Since my early retirement from service with the education department, to which I have already made reference, I had been in a kind of limbo. I had tried many things to fill the vacuum and even ended up for a while, somewhat ignominiously, back as a simple classroom teacher in the region of Fife.

Going back to the classroom was like putting on an old, familiar jacket: it felt comfortable and snug. Though Fife was on the opposite side of Scotland from where I started out and a different culture zone, I felt myself at home instantly. It was as if I had never been anywhere else. The kids were feisty and mischievous but warm and responsive and we had lots of laughs together.

I had always been a strong believer in the power of fun. I saw no reason why we, class and teacher, should not have a laugh, particularly in an English lesson. At the start of each new year with a class I used to say to them, "In the course of this year someone in this class is going to enjoy themselves. That's me! But, of course, you're welcome to join in." Though this was perceived and accepted as an invitation, they did not fail to realise that doing anything to disrupt this happy outcome was not exactly their best option.

I remember one classroom experience in Fife that exemplifies all this quite well.

We were studying a well-known short story by Roald Dahl. This story concerned a New York socialite who committed the seemingly perfect crime by ingeniously contriving the murder of her psychologically abusive husband whose dead body was found on the floor of a tampered-with lift when she had a perfect alibi.

We read this story together and then, to come to terms with its meaning and the complex motivations it contained and as a way of interrogating and taking full possession of the text, I set up the following scenario.

They were to imagine that, subsequently, the state became suspicious and the wife found herself in the dock accused of murder. The classroom would become a courtroom and the pupils would take up different roles in the drama, such as the accused wife, district attorney, public defender, judge, etc. They would improvise their roles using the text of the story as the basis for their role-play.

The pupils loved the excitement of taking part in a live drama that so resembled all those court cases that they had seen on TV. They entered into their parts with gusto, though there were too many m'luds for an authentic American court, if you ask me.

One girl in the class, who was not, in truth, the brightest of sparks, but fancied the glamour of the role, volunteered to be the court stenographer. There was no place for such a character in the original story, but it was not at all implausible in our reconstruction of the trial. So, we allowed it and she went on drumming happily with her fingers on the desk in front of her in pretend typing. After a while, the noise of her drumming became unbearably loud. I told her that this was a very modern court with an electric typewriter. Totally unphased, she went back to her 'typing' but with her fingers waggling silently in the air in front of her. And she kept this up for the whole duration of the 'trial'.

At one point, someone interrupted the drama to say, "Sir, Rosie's fell asleep. Will I waken her up?"

Rose Connelly, the girl in question, was a poor soul from a very deprived background and probably needed all the sleep she could get. Before I could say anything, one of the other players ingeniously said, "Naw. Dinnae waken her. She can play the deid body."

And so, when the time came for the policeman to give his evidence about finding the body of the husband in the lift, the pupil playing that role simply described the sleeping Rose, "His coat was torn and filthy and his hair looked as if it had been cut with an axe. He was well deid."

Rose did wake up later, only to receive a fantastic round of applause which pleased but mystified her exceedingly.

Many are the delicious stories I could tell of my reborn experience as a classroom teacher in Fife, like the Great Magic Mushroom Incident and our very dramatic and potentially disastrous visit to the Perth bull sales. Suffice to say, I felt tremendously reinvigorated to be back in front of a class.

However, it could be no more than a stopgap, the pause the cormorant takes on a rock to dry its wings. I needed a new challenge. Something that would have a future and would help me preserve my new-found sobriety.

Strangely, I saw the job with the VTU as doing all these things. I say 'strangely' because it was a job dealing with long-term unemployed people and I knew nothing about employment except having been employed all my life, which, I soon learned, was not the same thing at all. I had a good deal of the gallousness (cocky self-confidence to you) that I admired so much in the low-socio-economic pupils that I had always found most endearing. I thought, how hard could it be?

The team that formerly ran the VTU did not last long. After the defection of the manager, the rest left en masse soon after. Only one stayed on for a while but she did not feel at home in the new regime and soon followed her departed colleagues.

I think it was clear that they had run out of steam. Whatever belief they had had in the work had evaporated and the scheme itself was on the point of expiry. The records they left were scanty enough and did not provide a clear picture of what they were doing.

The basic premise of the scheme at that time was that the VTU should select applicants from the ranks of the officially registered unemployed, prioritising certain groups of the most vulnerable, for example, ex-drug addicts, ex-alcoholics, ex-criminal offenders and single mothers. These would be paid a weekly allowance just above the level of basic social benefit. Crucially, free childcare would be provided. After a brief period of preparation and assessment, they would be 'placed' with an employer for six months with the expectation that this would lead to permanent employment, the ultimate goal of the funding.

The value of this format to the employers was easy to see. They had workers on a (to them) free trial for a period of six months with no obligation to take them on the payroll. Of course, many did, but it was obviously a flaw in the scheme that the unit had to depend so heavily on the goodwill of the employers. What evidence there was from the previous administration suggested that their efforts were concentrated mainly on creating banks of amenable placement employers towards whom the clients of the VTU would be directed.

To me the greatest deficiency of this approach was the fact that it required you to look at the situation through the wrong end of the telescope. It meant fitting our clients, the poor and vulnerable people of the area, into jobs, any jobs, that were on offer rather than looking at what our clients had to offer and finding an outlet for this ambition in the job market.

A major change in thinking would be needed to reverse this imbalance. It would require a total revolution in the whole approach. How could we manage to achieve that?

The first problem we came up against was the sheer diversity of our population. The majority were women, mostly single mothers, but all came from a multitude of problematic backgrounds. They included the young and the old, the fresh-faced and the harrowed. Some had never worked in their lives, others had lost their jobs as a result of problems with alcohol or drugs, inability to accept authority, or pure fecklessness. Some were there through no fault of their own. They all had one thing in common. They all lacked self-confidence. Life had kicked them in the teeth once too often and they scarcely felt able any longer even to resent it.

The other great lack they had in that first intake was of education. Most of them had left school with no qualifications, no record of having ever even been there. Whether they had washed their hands of the school or whether it was the other way round need not concern us at this point. In the crucial matter of education, or more precisely the lack of it, I was convinced, lay the basis of their subsequent feelings of low self-worth and lack of confidence. I saw, only too clearly, that in some manner this deficit had to be addressed before we could direct them meaningfully into employment and towards economic and psychological independence.

Thus was born the People's College of Craigmillar.

SEVEN

The idea of the People's College did not arrive, fully formed, like sin out of the head of Satan. It was, rather, a slowly evolving concept. It depended on three major factors: firstly, the need for it as a vehicle for the regeneration of the mind and spirit of the participants; secondly, on its fitness for this purpose; and, finally and most critically, on the willingness of its co-creators, the people of Craigmillar, to embrace it.

This latter qualification was virtually assured, because the direness of their situation meant that our recruits would be prepared to try almost anything to improve their lot. This was reinforced by the inherent positivity of the inhabitants of this very deprived area which made them open to improvement.

By temperament the people of Craigmillar were easy-going and non-judgemental and so their mood was usually upbeat and friendly. Of course, like all human beings, they could fall out with each other from time to time but these flashpoints were isolated and short-term events. When it came to big issues like personal worth, life choices, morality or the lack of it, no one judged anyone negatively. I suppose, given their own imperfect backgrounds, they would not have had the cheek to do so.

As for the dreaded Gorgons of sexism, racism and religious intolerance, they never raised their ugly heads in the People's College. When people have real problems, such as getting enough money to pay the rent or putting food on a family table, they don't have the leisure for more trivial pursuits.

It is highly revealing that during the Troubles in Northern Ireland the only assemblies that Catholics and Protestants could safely attend together were meetings of Alcoholics Anonymous. This was because the alcoholics shared a common problem that was bigger, because more immediate in its personal consequences, than the political issues that divided the community. Even the paramilitaries on both sides recognised and respected this fact.

But even given their openness to improvement, it was clear that the majority of our intake were very far from being able, physically or psychologically, to step right into employment. They needed a period of recovery and rehabilitation before they would be ready to compete in the world of work. In some cases their minds would have to be recalibrated to adjust to the shock of having to face the prospect of a lifetime in employment.

Some people, I am aware, might respond to this by saying, 'poor dears!' or some such sarcastic put-down. But this would be unkind and unfair. The people who came to our door did not require or seek the condescending pity of anyone. They were tough people who wouldn't have come thus far if they had not already proved themselves to be resilient survivors. It was simply that they were momentarily down on their luck and needed only the encouragement of a helping hand to get themselves back on their feet again.

A second chance, if you like.

The key question was, how could we do this? How could we provide them with a period to recover their physical and mental energies, boost their self-confidence and provide them with the tools necessary to take that major step towards employability and self-sufficiency?

For several reasons I believed that the only way to do this was by a process of education or, more properly in this case, re-education. We must put them back to school!

This solution suggested itself to me for several reasons. First of all, because I was a teacher and no man forgets his trade but also because education, or the lack of it, was a large part of the problem, so it was logical to consider the possibility that it could be part of the solution.

Whether the school failed them or whether they failed the school was neither here nor there. On the surface they had emerged from the school with nothing, no certificates, no recognition of things learnt. Apparently they had gone through school as a fish glides through water, that is, seemingly without either disturbing it or being disturbed by it. I had the firm conviction, nearer to a faith, that this was not so.

No matter how uninteresting the lesson or how meagre the attention of the pupil, the process of education itself could not fail to leave some traces, however ghostly, on the learner. I was sure that these insubstantial remnants, if blown upon like embers, could be brought back to life.

The process of education we envisaged for them would be a classroom experience in which they would follow an appropriate curriculum of subjects, most of which would lead to certification, albeit at a modest level. In this way we would be rerunning their previous educational experience, only this time they would come out, not as losers, but as winners.

So, since we had the luxury of six months at our disposal, we decided to revamp the whole scheme by dedicating the first three months to formal re-education and training, including work-related training, on the premises which we now called the People's College. It was a name which we thought combined dignity with relevance. This period in the People's College, by now our training provider, would be followed by a similar period of three months in an appropriate job placement; for the intrinsic value of a period of placement or trial, in its own right, was something we had never denied.

So much for the theory, let us see how it panned out in practice.

The first problem that faced us in setting up this new structure was deciding what would be the curriculum in the school phase.

It went without saying that it would have to include English because many of our intake would have basic issues with reading and writing. Mathematics was also a must, because it provided a discipline, was useful in its own right, and was seen as part of the traditional core curriculum. (English and maths are the ham and eggs of education.)

We also included modern studies and a foreign language, in our case Spanish. This was a bit of swank on our part and included largely because these were traditionally studied only in the more academic classes in high school. We felt that it would signal our ambition for them, as well as our confidence in their ability to achieve such goals. It also gave the curriculum a more rounded feel, more like a traditional college.

It was obviously important that these subjects should lead to certification and we managed this through a link with one of the local further education centres whose expertise and participation in our venture proved invaluable. It widened our academic base, for one thing, and gave our trainees a sense of being part of a larger student world which intrigued and delighted them. It also motivated them immensely.

It was a street that ran two ways. The external tutor who provided our modern studies course, a teacher I had known previously from my days as an advisor whose name was Pete Smith, identified himself so closely with our philosophy and ideals as to become a member of the family rather than an adjunct to the staff. Pete contributed massively to the atmosphere we were trying to engender in the People's College and was much loved in return by all the trainees. If we had had the money we could have poached him from his day job – no problem!

I have previously stated that we chose to include a foreign language component in our curriculum for very good psychological reasons. However, the choice of Spanish as this language puzzles me still.

I have a very good command of Italian and you would think that I could have taught a course in this language myself. I rejected this possibility for two reasons: firstly, because it would have put an extra strain on my already onerous burden in managing the whole concept, on top of my other teaching responsibilities; and, secondly, because bringing in a tutor from the further education sector would add another new face to our staff and this would be of great advantage to us in expanding our base and enhancing the social breadth or compass of our project.

In the end, I suspect that the decision to opt for Spanish as our foreign language was the democratic decision of the students themselves. If they had any aspirations of a future foreign holiday (and for the most part they did not), then the venue for that holiday would probably have been Spain on account of its cheapness and relative accessibility.

However, in the end, no matter how we arrived at this decision, it turned out to be a good one. It was a positive delight to see these largely illiterate and unambitious people chatting away to each other in Spanish, even if of the most basic sort.

If the world-famous Scottish stand-up comic, Billy Connolly, had had the benefit of our Spanish course he might have spared himself the embarrassment he experienced in the following story he tells against himself.

He was holidaying in Spain and returning drunk night after night to his hotel, he was constantly being assailed by people shouting at him, "Buenas noches!" Not understanding this and mistaking it for an insult, he asks the concierge at his hotel what it means. The concierge explains that this means 'good evening' and that, far from being an insult, it is instead a polite and well-meaning expression of goodwill.

So, the following evening, returning from the beach, yet again in an elevated state of inebriation, he passes a cafe where a number of young men are congregating. Thinking to ingratiate himself with the locals he shouts over to the group, "Buenas noches," only to receive the reply, "Fuck off, ya Spanish bastard!"

One very important course that did not lead to certification was our course in creative writing. This arose out of my long-standing commitment to this activity. I had always believed in the value of creative writing at all levels in school since my very first days as a teacher.

Like Jean-Paul Sartre, the French writer and philosopher, I feel that people's lives are conducted for the most part in a series of short stories.

For most people the flow of life feels smooth and undifferentiated but for some it is consciously punctuated by shaped experiences that can be recognised and appreciated for their ability to give meaning to life. You can see this clearly at work in the ordinary, everyday manner in which people converse with each other. They recount what has happened to them essentially and naturally in the form of little anecdotes or short stories. 'You'll never guess what happened to me yesterday?'

By capturing these episodes in writing, though we are ostensibly only trying to tell a story, we are obliquely coming to terms with, and attempting to make sense of, nothing less than our own existence.

This emerges in the same way that the statue of David or the Pietà emerged from the stone that Michelangelo set out to carve. As he himself said, he didn't so much sculpt the block of marble into a statue as allow the work of art imprisoned in the cold stone to emerge from its confinement and, thus, reveal itself.

I firmly believe that everyone is capable of writing creatively, at their own level of competency, obviously. In this opinion I am at one with that great maker of paradoxes, G K Chesterton, who said somewhere that 'if a thing is worth doing, it is worth doing badly'.

This aphorism is, of course, not intended as some defence of shoddy workmanship. It merely means that if something is worth doing, you don't have to be the best in the world at it to derive pleasure and profit from it.

Think of the implications for tennis, for example, if this saying of Chesterton's were not so. Instead of millions of people getting enjoyment from playing the game at their own, sometimes bungling, level of competence, only the two very best tennis players on the planet would get the chance to play against each other. One long interminable game to the utter boredom of all.

I hope it will not seem self-indulgent if I break off at this point to tell a little story that concerns my own mother. I feel that this is well justified because it serves as a very effective objective correlative of the power of the creative urge, as well as the universality of its endowment.

The ability and the ambition to write creatively does not always occur in the usual places: it strikes, apparently randomly, where it will and can.

There can never be too many writers, just as there can never be too many published authors. Every published work of any merit whatsoever has its own particular value, creates its own taste and fills its own space, however miniscule, in the vast pantheon of literature.

My mother was a typical working-class wife and mother of the war years. She was a stay-at-home mum who was always there for us, literally and metaphorically, come what may.

Years later, when my two younger brothers and I were married and left home – and, in my case, the area – and, after the death of my father, my mother, still a very active woman, went back to work to supplement her niggardly widow's pension.

She had been 'in service' in her youth which meant that she was working as a domestic in the houses of the rich and landed in the outlying area. When she became a widow she took a job as a hospital cleaner. This job, though humble enough, suited my mother's personality greatly. She was a very gregarious person who liked nothing better than to chat to people. Of course, this is a very welcome characteristic in someone who works in a hospital.

My mother knew many of the patients already, but even the ones she didn't know previously soon yielded to the force of her amiability and lively good nature and became friends. My mother had a great talent for chatting to strangers. It was one of her ways of widening her horizons.

When she had to retire from this job, she entered a period of bad health and suffered a series of heart attacks which she, miraculously, survived.

After her fifth heart attack the surgeon told me, "Your mother is like an old alarm clock. When it stops, we manage to get it going again by giving it a bit of a shake. One day that shake will not be enough to bring your mother back to life."

And so it proved to be. She died as a result of her seventh heart attack. As well as precipitating us into the most intense grief, this event led to the discovery of an extraordinary secret life on the part of our mother of which my brothers and I had no knowledge.

After my mother's death we received a great many Mass cards and messages of condolence and sympathy. Amongst these latter, we came across a letter from a total stranger who identified himself as the literary editor of the *Glasgow Herald*, one of the two most prestigious broadsheets in Scotland. After expressing his deep sorrow at the passing of my mother, he said an extraordinary thing.

Your mother, he said, *was a writer of rare quality*.

Our mother? A writer? Of rare quality? What was he talking about? Surely, there was some mistake here?

But there was no mistake. Under my mother's bed we discovered, hidden, an old, battered, zip-round suitcase. It was stuffed with handwritten manuscripts, fragments of autobiography, stories and anecdotes of local life, poems and, especially, hymns, for my mother was a very devout woman.

It turned out that, though we did not know about her secret life as a writer, it was well known to the 'sisterhood', her female friends and neighbours, young and old, in the high-rise apartment block she stayed in before her death. They all used to meet up, apparently, in the laundry room in the basement where my mother would read to them from her latest works.

In fact, that is what she was doing when she had her fatal heart attack. She had been invited by her parish pensioners' group to address them on the subject of her writing.

This must have been an astonishingly big occasion for my mother, given the humble nature of her roots and her total lack of experience of public speaking. She must have been, as she herself would have said, 'up to high doh' with excitement and apprehension.

Anyway, a few minutes into her talk my mother fell down dead. The excitement proved too much for her. The group of sixty or so pensioners that were present immediately fell to their knees and began to recite the Rosary. Someone went for the priest, just across the lawn. He arrived and my mother was given the Last Rites almost before her soul had time to leave her body.

All during the period of my mother's recurring heart attacks, she had had one great fear. It wasn't of dying itself; her faith was too strong for that. It was of having a fatal attack in the friendless public street or being found lying shamefully undiscovered in some bushes. To cope with this fear, my mother developed a great devotion to St Joseph for the gift of a happy death. After all, St Joseph is the patron saint of a happy death since he died, we may confidently presume, in the arms of Jesus and his beloved mother, Mary.

I never discovered the basis of the literary editor's good opinion of my mother's work or how it came to his attention. There was nothing of it published, so far as I know. It did turn out that she was a member of a local creative writing group. This connection may have led to knowledge of her work spreading as far as the literary pages of the *Glasgow Herald*. It remains still a mystery. I am ashamed to say that at the time of my mother's death and after it I was too absorbed with the drink and its faithful companion, self-pity, to conduct the enquiries that would have been necessary to solve the mystery. Mea culpa, mea culpa, mea maxima culpa.

EIGHT

A major problem I encountered in my early-career efforts to encourage creative writing was that school pupils are, by and large, reluctant to write anything! They will talk, endlessly, and read, if they have to, but they have a real aversion to writing. It feels too much like work. This is particularly true of the less academically inclined pupils.

Fortunately, as a young teacher starting out, my head was full of innovative ideas and I had the energy and audacity to put them into practice. One of these ideas centred on finding a way to deal with and overcome this aversion to writing itself.

To this end, I used to bring into the classroom an old-fashioned tape recorder and some tapes of suitable music to play only when they were writing. The music, I discovered, had to be carefully chosen. It couldn't be exciting or dramatic. So, no popular music. The ideal music, I found, was Mozart or Bach or light classical music. This produced the effect of a trickling fountain at the back of the room and was marvellously conducive to creating a mood of serenity and calmness. For most of the pupils this oasis of peace and tranquillity was in stark contrast to the noisy confusion of their lives outside of the classroom.

And they loved it!

There were many occasions on which, if it seemed that the class hadn't been writing for some time, someone would pipe up and say, "Whit aboot that writin', sir? When ur we gettin' back tae that?" I do not delude myself: it wasn't so much that they were missing the writing but, rather, the tranquillity that went with it.

Another practical advantage of this innovation was the fact that the music mopped up and obliterated all the other little sounds that distract in a classroom; the sounds of distant traffic, the coughing and sneezing and the shuffling of feet. It absorbed all of these noises like blotting paper and induced an almost monastic silence in the room which aided their work enormously.

At the same time, it must be said, the other teachers who had occasion to visit my room during these sessions, including some very senior staff, were disconcerted by the spectacle. When they came into an English classroom where the pupils, as it appeared to them, were just listening to music rather than working, it greatly disturbed and, even, offended them. It seemed as if I was having a good time to myself and the pupils were being deprived of the hard graft it was my duty to impose on them.

But they could not have been more deluded. In fact I was getting wonderful work out of the class. They were producing pieces of work which were vivacious and imaginative – and profoundly liberating. The range of their creativity was amazing. They told charming and affecting stories about their childhood and family life. They related fantastic tales of strange, extra-terrestrial creatures and other phantoms that threatened life on Earth. Most popular of all were their stories of real-life adventure and derring-do, mostly centred on autobiographical episodes of delinquency or malfeasance. I swear I could have solved half the juvenile crime in the area from their fiction alone.

In the end my colleagues' narrow-mindedness gave way to a grudging acceptance and they left us alone.

In this fecund period of my probationary two years, this was not the only one of my innovations that gave even my close friends on the staff cause for question and concern.

I had read somewhere a statistic that had a devastating effect on me. It appeared from this statistic that a surprisingly large number of children at any given time in school suffer from a range of problems, such as hunger, lack of sleep arising from chaotic family circumstances, sexual abuse and other serious forms of neglect. These shattered pupils are expected to turn up at school and pretend that everything in the garden is lovely. They do this so effectively that it is virtually impossible for the teacher to tell which pupils, at any given time, are so shattered as to be in no position, mentally or physically, to derive any benefit from the lesson.

Accepting the truth of this research and translating it into my own classroom situation, it meant that between two and three pupils – in every one of my classes! – were in no fit state, for one reason or another, to concentrate their attention on what was happening in the classroom.

Here is what I decided to do about it.

I got the janitor to set up a pinboard that ran along the back of my room. In front of this I set up a trestle table with two pairs of scissors, two jars of paste with brushes and a big pile of carefully chosen glossy magazines of the type of *National Geographic* (so, nothing indecent or inflammatory of teenage hormones).

I let it be known to the class that if anyone didn't feel up to taking part in the lesson for any unspecified reason, they were free to simply withdraw, without explanation, to the back of the room and spend their time during the lesson in cutting out random images from the magazines provided and pasting them on the roll of paper with which I had covered the pinboard. Only a maximum of two at a time were permitted to take advantage of this digression. It would be left to themselves to decide who had most need of this respite. Furthermore, I made it clear to them that what appeared on the wall would remain private and I would not ever look at it. I guessed very well that, human nature being what it is, the work of art that developed over time would become a means of making a collective, artistic statement of their discontent, anger and powerlessness. I regarded this creative aspect of what was basically a cut-and-paste form of time-passing as a great compensation.

Of course, all my friends on the staff told me it would never work; that the same people would be opting out all the time and this would be detrimental to their own education as well as making a fool of my good-natured but misguided altruism.

I was able to assure them that this never happened. The scheme regulated itself perfectly, based on the natural sense of justice that, in my experience, few classes lack. If anyone attempted to take advantage of the situation at the expense of someone more needy, the mood of the class would quickly turn against them. A spokesperson for the group would brusquely tell him 'to sit on his arse' or words to that effect and point to someone else to take his place, someone that was known to them, but obviously not to me, as being more deserving of the break.

I was, of course, massively intrigued by the artwork that developed impressively over the year but I kept my word to them and did not look closely at the work. All I could see from my position at the front of the class were broad swatches of colour that seemed to move and whorl across the composition like the images of fractal geometry.

I continued to resist the temptation to look even after one of my closest friends asked me if, by chance, I had looked recently at the detail of the work on the pinboard at the back of my room. I told him that, no, I hadn't. With an arch look on his face, he drily said, "Well, I think it's time you did. There's a lot of shit happening on that board, including something pretty unsavoury involving the Queen and a bottle of HP sauce."

Returning to the People's College, creative writing became a mainstream activity and yielded great fruits individually and collectively. Our students gained in self-awareness and confidence and the group as a whole became more closely bonded as a result of listening to each other's stories which were always dramatic and colourful as well as, where appropriate, extremely funny. The single greatest quality of communities like the Vennel or Craigmillar is their ability to laugh themselves out of their misery.

As you would expect many of the female trainees in the creative writing sessions opted to tell stories with a strong romantic flavour. These were, of course, never of the type of cheap romantic novels with their strong emphasis on the conventional and the polite. They were hard-hitting and real stories of love and its complications. But frank though they were, they were never in any sense sexually explicit or titillating. I suppose this was out of respect for me who would be reading them.

Their delicacy in this regard stands in sharp contrast to my experience of reading female fiction when I was a marker for the Scottish Examination Board during my time as a principal teacher of English.

An essential part of the English Higher exam was an element of extended or free writing called the 'essay'. This important part of the rubric of the exam offered the candidate a choice of different styles or forms of writing on which to write their essay; for example, an account of a hobby or interest, a critical evaluation of some controversial issue, a piece of pure descriptive writing or a short piece of fiction on some suggested theme.

One of the surprising outcomes of my work as a marker was the discovery that around three in every hundred essays contained what could only be described as smut. This was almost always produced by girls. I cannot explain why this is. I suppose you can understand the temptation. It is a stressful time for hormonal teenagers, the atmosphere of the examination hall is fetid, you are all alone at your seat in front of an invigilator you do not know and will never see again. What you are writing will forever remain secret; it will never be seen by your teacher or anyone you know, only by some distant and anonymous marker.

But why it should be predominantly, almost exclusively, girls that succumb in these circumstances to the temptation to produce pornography is beyond my ability to explain. To complicate things further, I would go as far as to say that most times, it was the more intelligent types of girls who did this.

The example of this that follows may prove very revealing, in more ways than one.

The Highers examination was the pinnacle of academic achievement in what was called the secondary or high school. It was, amongst other things, the major means of accessing university. The team of markers that were assembled for judging the English Higher were recruited mainly from those principal teachers who had gained their experience through teaching in some of the most successful schools in Scotland. As such, they were usually very conservative in their views of what constituted a good answer. They thought of themselves as guardians of the standards of good English and God help anyone who failed to meet their strict criteria. Their zeal and ferocity in defending what they saw as 'The Tradition' could not be faulted, but, in truth, imagination and originality did not rate with them very highly as virtues in writing. You could say that in this respect they catered mainly for that particular group that I called in an earlier part of this work the 'good-at-school', those who knew best how to exploit the system.

I had been invited to join the markers' team, unusually, on the basis of some sterling successes I had achieved at this level with pupils from very deprived backgrounds. I suppose my election could be seen as an honest attempt on the part of the Scottish Examination Board to widen their net. At least, a little!

We, prospective markers, used to be called together, before we started marking the scripts, to look at some sample scripts, already graded provisionally by the senior examiners. The idea behind this was to give us the opportunity to discuss these scripts and, thus, align our own marking with accepted models. This was to ensure consistency across the whole cohort of examinees.

In the course of one markers' meeting we were presented with a script which we were asked to evaluate. The script had been written in response to the rubric that offered the possibility of writing about a hobby or interest.

The candidate, that the internal evidence soon revealed to be a girl or young woman, entitled her piece HAND-GLIDING. It was intended to mislead the slipshod reader into thinking that it read HANG-GLIDING. And it worked! It soon became obvious that the majority of markers in the room, mostly retired, mainly female, principal teachers, thought they were reading an essay about the sport of hang-gliding rather than an essay about hand-gliding or masturbation.

It was an extremely clever spoof and it is not at all surprising that it deceived so many people. In the end, the majority verdict was that it merited a B+.

It was at this point that a teacher from a comprehensive school in Glasgow, mistakenly thinking the script had been included for that particular reason, piped up and said, "What about the pornography? Whit ur we supposed tae make o' that?"

There was an immediate outburst of shock in the room.

"What are you talking about? What pornography?" exploded one of the more elderly ladies, whose flowery hat was shedding petals as she shook her head in outrage at the very suggestion. The young Glasgow teacher very patiently said, "Dae ye want me tae draw ye a picture, hen?"

He then went on to explain how so many of the words and phrases in the piece had a cleverly ambiguous, but, nonetheless, clear reference to masturbation. He pointed, as an example, to the first sentence which read, *I have always longed to take myself up to the top of a very high hill and toss myself off.* Then he pointed out that the club she speaks of joining in order to further her interest in this hobby was called, revealingly, Hancock's Hand-Gliding Club.

His case was irrefutable and soon the very ladies that were aghast at the very idea of such conduct on the part of a Higher's candidate, far less a female one, began calling for the script to be deemed an outright fail on grounds of indecency.

Of course, it was pointed out that this could never be allowed. We were there to judge the quality of the English (and it was undeniable in this case), not the morals of the writer. Eventually, an untidy and irrational compromise was reached and her mark was reduced from a B+ to a C.

All that had passed merely emphasised the clever nature of the writing and I had no doubt that if I were to be presented with a script like that in my markers' bundle, I would give it an outright A.

NINE

Getting back to the People's College, with the system now in place, the only thing that remained was to sell this concept to our shareholders, that is, our clients, now called students; to our immediate bosses in the Craigmillar Festival Society; to the Edinburgh Council officials who oversaw our management of the scheme; and, finally, to the supervisors of the European Social Fund, our co-funders.

The students loved it and embraced it immediately. They rather liked being sat at a desk again. It brought back happy memories of carefree schooldays and made them feel young again. They fairly ate up the work and became visibly excited by it. The bustle and joy of our schoolroom greatly enlivened all who witnessed it.

My bosses in the Craigmillar Festival Society accommodated themselves to the idea without too much difficulty because they had implicit faith in me and were intrigued and, in a way, flattered by the possibility that we could achieve something so revolutionary. Naming our college the People's College was very attractive to them, politically.

The supervisors of the European Social Fund posed no problem because they were quite remote from us and were chiefly concerned with such matters as our fulfilment of the strict recruitment quotas; with the financial management of the scheme; and, most of all, with our exit success in the form of jobs. This data was supplied to them annually by means of a long and comprehensive report on all aspects of our functioning. We fulfilled all the criteria strictly and were rendered immune from criticism because we went on to have an 85% success rate, year on year, in finding permanent employment for our students.

The only problem that we encountered, at first, was with our immediate bosses, the council officials of the local authority. These were highly sceptical of the whole idea of the People's College to begin with. This was partly because it was in some sense a revolutionary concept. We were, consciously, taking a step back to take several steps forward. Still, this was to some counter-intuitive and that means to a bureaucrat utterly beyond comprehension. Their approval was absolutely necessary to get the funding without which the scheme would come to an abrupt end. We had to fight them tooth and nail before they finally gave their, still reluctant, consent.

In this struggle for our very existence the support of the Craigmillar Festival Society was absolutely vital and the two locally elected councillors, who had appointed me in the first place, were very strong allies in this struggle. Personally and politically, they carried a lot of weight in the council and proved too strong in the end for the paltry pen-pushers beneath them in the political and administrative chain of command.

I always thought that on the part of the council staff (quite senior officers I might add) there was a tinge of resentment, almost a twisted sort of class-based envy, that we were showing so much confidence in the educational improvability of this very deprived group in a very disadvantaged community. It flew in the face of all their social prejudices. I think that they might also have considered it a piece of dubious self-indulgence on my part. Either way, I took the opposition of the naysayers as a backhanded compliment and didn't let it bother me in the slightest.

I said just now that the system was in place. However, it would be more accurate to say that the educational part of our system was in place, for by now the People's College was fairly steaming ahead like a train full of happy and excited holidaymakers at the beginning of the Glasgow Fair Fortnight.

However, the total package still lacked two key ingredients.

One, obviously, was the inclusion of an element of preparation-for-work training. This would have to cover such things as the construction of a CV, some job interview training and the acquiring of a good work ethic, all of which I will deal with separately later. But not before I deal with the second key ingredient of our programme which constituted our greatest innovation and presented our most formidable challenge. This was our incorporation into the curriculum of a course on Cosmology. This puzzled many, even amongst our supporters, but caught the attention of the wider world, including the academic world, in a way that surprised everyone but me.

TEN

My interest in cosmology began several years before I came to the Vocational Training Unit and arose, by way of extension, from my acceptance of the theory of evolution as the most likely hypothesis for the development of life on Earth.

Despite, or more accurately because of, being a committed Catholic, I never had the slightest difficulty in accepting evolution as the most plausible agency for the formation of species. I never felt bound, even for a moment, to accept the proposition of the Christian fundamentalists that, since the Bible is unerring, only the literal story of how life arrived on Earth, as described in the *Book of Genesis*, is true and that, therefore, all the species on Earth were created simultaneously in all their diversity in the course of only six days.

God is, even by their own definition and mine, an all-powerful spirit without beginning or end. As such, he is outside of time and space and could not be constrained by either. So, whether the world was created in a nanosecond, in six days, or over the course of billions of years, is theologically immaterial.

By the same token I am not at all impressed by the militant atheists, like Richard Dawkins, who never tire of telling us that there is no God and that those who believe that there is, are no more than dolts, or worse.

They may claim that they see no evidence for the existence of such a being. They may even say that there is no need for such a being to explain Creation and everything that is in it. Both of these statements are perfectly rational up to a point. However, they take a step too far when they say, definitively, that God does not exist.

There is no possible way for them, as scientists, of proving such a proposition. God, being by definition pure spirit, could not in any circumstances be subject to physical proof or experiment. Therefore their denial of any possibility of there being a God is, not to put too fine a point on it, simply an unscientific assertion, an article of faith or belief, if you like. It makes them little more than votaries of a non-God-believing cult.

Better for the moment to just leave God out of the equation. Science works perfectly well whether you believe in God or don't.

Before I go any further in this enterprise I must issue a disclaimer. In my schooldays I was the epitome of a pure arts student. I was a total incompetent in the science or maths aspects of the curriculum, in fact famously so.

I remember my old maths teacher, at my nth example of gross stupidity, asking me in front of the class, "McLaughlin (the public school formality of using surnames was common at that time, even in the state schools)," he said, "tell me, can you sing?"

Innocently, I replied that in fact I was a very good singer with some reputation locally as a soloist.

Irritably waving aside my self-justification, he said, "That's as may be, but you'll still need a monkey if you're ever going to earn a living!"

He was referring to the phenomenon of the very popular itinerant street-singers of the time, that I told you about earlier, who enjoyed most success in their trade when they had a monkey, with a cute little red jacket and cap, to climb up the drainpipes and collect donations from the windows higher up in the tenements of the area.

He was also implying that I would prove to be a great failure in school and in later life.

Strangely, I was not in the slightest bit hurt or damaged by this utter dismissal of my scholastic abilities. This for two reasons: firstly, because I rather liked the man who was good-natured in a bluff sort of way; and, secondly, because I did not mind in the slightest not being good at maths or any other of the sciences. These were subjects for swots who could scarcely put two words together. Rather than taking his dismissive opinion of my mathematical talent as an insult, in some twisted way, I took it as a compliment.

Sadly, I am bound to say that his ill-opinion of my mathematical ability was proved only too justified in the end. After years of studying maths and science, I emerged from school with only a Lower maths to show for it. This was as low a qualification as you could get – and I only got that at the second attempt.

You can readily see that I was ill-fitted by temperament and training to make much sense of a heavily science-based enterprise such as the study of cosmology. Nevertheless I was drawn to it as the snake is to the eyes of the mongoose. I was fascinated by the night sky and the mysteries contained in those myriad twinkling dots of light. I wanted to know how deep was space and what those lights represented, of what they were made, where they came from and where they were going.

So, innocent as a baby, I decided to wade in and read everything I could lay my hands on that would answer my questions.

My study was desultory to say the least. I just read whatever came to hand, when it came to hand, in any order, on any uncoordinated aspect of the subject. Thus I read books on Chaos Theory, fractals, quasars, galaxy formation, quantum mechanics. I read about stellar Red Giants and Brown Dwarves, about Black Holes and Wormholes and the marvellously named String Theory.

When I say I read them, let me be quite plain. I could not by any means claim that I understood them in any fundamental sense. However, by persistence I managed to acquire some broad ideas or pictures of the key aspects of the subject.

I knew that it all began, probably, with the Big Bang which can be imagined as an explosive event in which from what is called a Singularity (a Singularity is an entity that has virtually no dimensions but almost infinite density) sprang forth the whole cosmos with its billions of stars in trillions upon trillions of galaxies and nebulae with names like Andromeda, Orion, Cat's Eye, Horsehead, Hourglass and our own Milky Way, of course. How I loved, not the science, but the magic of all that. This was not the stuffy halls of academe; this was Narnia.

I used the word 'probably' with reference to the Big Bang Theory advisedly. This is because in the world of science there are many things that cannot be replicated and tested – and, therefore, proved to be indisputably true. This holds true in the study of the very large structures of the universe, which is called cosmology, as well as in the study of the exceedingly small at the atomic and subatomic level, which is governed by the laws of quantum mechanics.

The theory of the Big Bang as an explanation of how the universe came to be, though now accepted by the majority of scientists, is only one of many alternative theories for the origin of the cosmos. Some of these are held by crackpots with an inclination towards science fiction but also by, in some cases, respected cosmologists, like the celebrated Fred Hoyle. Since the conditions that led to the creation of the universe are remote by 15 billions of years and cannot be proved to be true in an absolute sense, we are compelled to accept them – or not – on the basis of educated conjecture or probability.

In the domain of the very small that deals with atoms and particles the situation is even more complex and unfathomable. It is a world where many bizarre and spooky things happen (I borrow the word 'spooky' from Einstein, that towering giant of modern physics, who used it in this very context to describe the inexplicably strange things that happen in the world of quantum mechanics). Elementary particles behave in ways that defy logic and seem more akin to metaphysics or magic than conventional science.

Take, for example, what I call 'the ghostly quantum leap'.

Inside the atom from time to time the electron suddenly changes its orbit around the nucleus. It does this in a way that almost defies belief. It does not traverse or move across the space between one orbit and the other, as common sense would dictate. Instead, it just ceases to exist in one orbit and simultaneously reappears in another, like some spiritual apparition. It is as if you were to suddenly pop out of existence wherever you are now and reappear in a strange place, perhaps thousands of miles away, with no way of knowing how you got there. It's the stuff of *Star Trek*, is it not?

I call this enigma number one.

Then there is the fact that quantum mechanics indulges in a bit of shape-shifting in the manner of a Hollywood horror movie. A quantum of energy can manifest itself, apparently arbitrarily, in quite different forms; sometimes as a particle and sometimes as a wave. We know this for a fact because it has been confirmed by experiment in the laboratory.

What we do not know is how or why this happens. It is as if a prowling shark were to suddenly turn itself into a sparkling shoal of small fish and then back again at will. This leaves us with a basically philosophical question. Is this a shark that turns itself into a shoal of fish or is it a shoal of fish that can turn into a shark? Or is it some hypostatic union between shark and shoal like that between God and man in Jesus? It is a question science cannot – and possibly never could – answer.

This is enigma number two.

The third example I will give – and enigma number three – is what I call 'seeing is behaving'.

It concerns the role of the observer in quantum mechanics. It seems that in the world of quantum mechanics things behave in one way when we are looking at them and in an entirely different way when they are unobserved.

Of course, this is by way of a truism in ordinary life. Everyone has had the experience of making an embarrassing mistake just because someone was watching them perform some task. This is an altogether different proposition and can be explained on the basis of simple psychology.

Harder to believe is the possibility that in the objective world of quantum mechanics the behaviour of phenomena can be affected by the simple fact that they are being looked at whether by an operative or by his or her equipment. And yet, this has been confirmed to be so in the laboratory, specifically in experiments carried out in Israel by Professor Mordechai Heiblom and his team. No one knows the underlying reason for this happening: they can detect it but not explain it. Suffice to say that it is strange enough to be scary.

It seems that in the world of quantum mechanics the only thing that we know for sure is that, as the graffiti artist might put it, 'Uncertainty Rules. OK!'.

In the course of my cosmological studies I learned that our planet is part of the Solar System and that our sun is one of more than a billion such stars in our Milky Way Galaxy which is, in turn, one amongst trillions of galaxies in the total universe. In other words the cosmos is big – big beyond imagining. If we were capable of building a spacecraft that could travel at a million miles an hour, it would take us three thousand years to get only as far as our nearest neighbouring star, Alpha Centauri.

And yet, on this tiny planet circumnavigating a minor star, life has emerged and produced human beings that can think, examine and contemplate. It is an awe-inspiring and puzzling concept. How did we get from that almost massless Singularity (for the purposes of this book I am going with the Big Bang Theory) to the vast panoply of stars, galaxies and nebulae without number that led to the emergence of thinking human beings? The number of coincidences and fortunate chance events that were necessary to produce this miracle are simply mind-blowing. And yet it happened – and we are here to prove it!

The next question follows logically and fast on the heels of the question of how we came to be. It is this. Are we alone in the cosmos or are there other beings, almost certainly more advanced, that exist in some far-flung part of the cosmos that are looking at us right now and, presumably, shaking their heads.

Surprisingly, the question as to whether we are the only intelligent life in the cosmos is still an open question. Many scientists, following the law of averages, say that intelligent life must have emerged elsewhere in the cosmos, astonishingly vast and thronged as it is, perhaps many times, even if taking very different forms from life on Earth. Others say that the emergence of life on Earth was the result of so many incredible chance events and coincidences that it is possible to imagine that ours is the only planet to have managed the progression to intelligent life.

Cosmology was indeed a very complicated subject, full of many baffling and unknowable elements that still puzzle the greatest scientific minds of modern times. So why did I even consider introducing it into our curriculum, especially given my own tenuous grasp of its complexities? What possible good would it be to my long-term unemployed clients?

Well, first of all, I believe, with Socrates, that the unexamined life is not worth living. My trainees had a right to know who they were, and how they came to be, not only as individuals, but as a species.

Furthermore, for people who lacked confidence it would provide the opportunity to see themselves as intensely significant, as the offspring of gigantic cosmic forces. This would allow them to leapfrog the barriers of class, poverty and social disadvantage, those mere accidents of the human condition, and grow in self-confidence and worth.

At a stroke it would have the happy effect of exterminating those large-scale demons, such as racism, sexism, homophobia and religious intolerance which are endemic in human society. After all, if we, as individuals, are cosmically significant, so is every other individual on the planet without exception for we are all the product of the same physical and evolutionary forces.

On the basis of my profound belief as a teacher that anything can be taught to any learner at some level so long as the learner's capabilities and level of development are taken into account, I felt confident that even my necessarily simplistic account of cosmology would bear some fruit in the cloisters of our little college. After all, we can, and do, teach simple theology, called by some 'the Queen of the sciences', to mere children.

I was heartened in this optimism by an experience I had with a class of similarly disadvantaged pupils in those very fecund probationary years of my early teaching experience. I think their story is worth telling, in the chapter that follows, for its own sake, as well as for the light it throws on my later experience in the People's College. It has an extra-terrestrial twist to it which is a happy accident.

ELEVEN

The major piece of work I am going to describe started out as a routine exercise in creative writing. The class concerned was 3E which in the hierarchical structure of the school meant that they were well below the level of the highest-achieving academic classes but above the level of the most intellectually deprived. They were a difficult class of very tough boys with enough native cunning to give you all the trouble you could wish for, if you rubbed them up the wrong way.

I had the good fortune to get on really well with them, so they accepted, readily enough, my suggestion that we should write a play. For some reason this idea appealed to them. When I tentatively suggested to them that we might even perform it in public, they were locked in. These kids were nothing, if not natural-born show-offs.

Early on it was established that the whole project would be a collective enterprise: one in which I would be an equal member with them, both in the creation of the play and its subsequent bringing to the stage.

It was decided that the plot should be based on the story of Noah from the Bible but updated. Noah became Dr Noah who was a very high-placed scientist working at a military/industrial complex. His involvement in this work greatly troubles his conscience. So, when he begins to receive radio messages from some remote source in outer space telling him that the earth was about to be destroyed in an impending calamity, he is only too happy to quit his job at the base and begins building a rocket to allow him and his family to escape the catastrophe to come.

The play, we collectively determined, would be in three acts. Act One would concern itself with events leading up to the cataclysm. Act Two would deal with the time spent travelling in space. Act Three would see the drama resolved with their arrival at their destination.

Act One gave the opportunity to explore the reactions of all the relevant parties to Dr Noah's strange obsession with building this rocket. His wife was unquestioningly supportive. The sons, on the other hand, were highly sceptical about this tale of a mysterious space voice, called Ogd, that was leading their father to make a fool of himself and a mockery of them. Their cachet value had plummeted when their father had given up his job at the base to pursue this ludicrous obsession. His neighbours and friends were openly derisory of him. Amongst his neighbours there were some who expressed their resentment at the fact that he was doing all this to benefit his own family at the expense of everyone else. This was irrational, given that they were convinced that he was delusional, if not well and truly mad, and was probably based on the fact that, laugh though they might, a little part of them worried about the tiny possibility that he could be right.

In Act Two the family find themselves in space. They have no idea where they are going and have no means of influencing the direction of travel. What particularly angers the sons is the fact that control of their lives has been taken from them. As one of the sons says at one point in the play:

"How come there's nae windaes (windows) in this thing? We cannae even see where wur goin'. Fur aw we know we could still be sittin' like bampots back home in oor ain gairden wi' aw the neebours runnin' roon aboot us laffin' ther heeds aff."

Philosophic, or what?

Act Three sees them arrive on a blasted planet devoid of vegetation. It is a wasted, desolate region but, surprisingly, the sons are enormously excited by the opportunity this barren world offers to them to make a world for themselves, in their own image, so to speak, and start frantically exploring their new environment. Two of the sons rush off to investigate some stunted growths that they see, or imagine that they see, in the far distance.

The play comes to an end when one of the scouting party rushes in to say, "We've found trees, apple trees. And they're alive!" This subtle recall of the Garden of Eden where it all went wrong the first time round was not lost on the simple, but religiously aware, mainly Catholic, audience that we attracted for the performance.

How we brought all this to paper is interesting. We would talk (incessantly) around suggested scenes, mainly conversations. For example, father with son, husband with wife, sons with friends, neighbour to neighbour. At the conclusion of these discussions we would have a number of great ideas and some cracking vocabulary.

The class then had to write something about anything that appealed to them in the discussion. It could be as little as a couple of words or as long as they liked. At the end of the session we would collect all these random scribblings and keep the ideas, words and expressions that we liked and discard the rest. Thus by a process of trial and error and constant refinement we ended up with a script.

In this respect the case of one of our number, Joe Carr, is highly revealing.

By this time, the group had decided to move our work on the play away from its allotted slot in the official school timetable and to work on it every day in their own lunch hour. This surprising decision was taken partly because they were becoming excited by it and wanted to keep up the pace but partly because doing it in their own time was an anti-authoritarian gesture and would give them more freedom to express themselves.

Anyway to get back to Joe Carr. Joe was a compulsive truant who hated school and couldn't abide the claustrophobia it induced in him. He spent his days alone on the golf course.

Out of the blue, Joe took to appearing at our clandestine lunchtime sessions and leaving immediately afterwards. To do this secretly and without the inevitable repercussions if he were discovered, Joe used to climb, unseen, the steep cliff at the back of the school, a serious climb, if you ask me. He would enter through the big classroom window and, magically, appear amongst us like Jesus to the Apostles at Emmaus.

With him he would bring screeds of writing on which he had occupied himself among the dunes of the golf course. (I had kept him supplied with notebooks, undoubtedly as a sop to my conscience.) Each time Joe arrived he would say, exultantly, "Hello, guys, ah've got yer play for yous." Unfortunately, most of what Joe produced was rubbish and we never found a use for it.

Then one day, unusually, with his meanderings he included a slip of paper with nothing more than two words on it. The words were 'apple trees'. Funnily enough, these words became, as we have already discovered, the most important words in the whole play and were the words that brought the curtain down at its conclusion.

Tellingly, the boys decided to call their play *The Second Chance*.

Once we had a script we became thoroughly engaged in all aspects of bringing it to the stage. The venue would obviously be the school hall but we needed to consider all the other factors that would contribute to the performance, such as scenery, props and stage effects.

In addition we had to deal with the business side of such a project, like design and pricing of tickets, advertising and sales.

It turned out that the majority of the boys in our collective were born entrepreneurs and the business side worked perfectly; in fact, too perfectly, one could say. The collective had decided to price the tickets at £5 each, an enormous price at that time, not only for a school show. I strenuously objected that this price was far too high but I was easily outvoted. The tickets sold like hot cakes (they were excellent ticket touts). On the night of the performance they decided to open a cash gate for anyone that turned up without tickets. I immediately protested that this was unethical, probably illegal and would certainly breach health and safety regulations.

They told me not to worry.

"Efter aw," they said, "these tickets wur sold ages ago and wid've been stuck at the back o' the picture of the Sacred Heart on the mantelpiece and forgot aboot. Lots of people that bought tickets will no' turn up. By opening a paygate we're jist makin' sure we get a fuull hoose."

And a full house is precisely what we got.

The play proved to be a great success, theatrically, and ended to wild acclamation. At one point in the play in Act Two when the sons of Dr Noah are questioning the blind nature of their journey and their lack of personal control of their destiny, two priests, out of a contingent of twenty-five or so from the local deanery, walked out, noisily, in protest at what they felt was unwarranted questioning of matters of faith. Their protest had the single effect of making them seem a bit ridiculous. However, when I think about it, I rather admire them for their action, for though words like faith or God were nowhere mentioned in the play, these priests had perfectly grasped the underlying and, in my opinion, healthy scepticism that lay at the heart of the work.

In anticipation of the first performance, because of the great uncertainty of its outcome and possible repercussions, even my closest friends on the staff had kept a severe distance from me and I was left quite alone with only my little collective as support.

After the play proved to be such a great success, there was a huge sense of excitement and, on my part, relief that it had all gone so well.

Financially, its success was almost embarrassing, for, taking into account the initial sale of tickets, the cash takings on the night and the proceeds from a cafeteria that the boys had enterprisingly set up, we were positively awash with money. I remember vividly how after the performance people kept coming up to me and pressing cash into my hands. My pockets were fairly bursting with half-crowns and ten-bob notes. At one point an urchin came up to me and thrust a fistful of coins at me. I did not know the boy and suspect that he didn't even come from our school. In my bumbling middle-class way I said to him as he was rushing away, "Wait a minute, son, here's something for yourself." He grinned at me and said, "It's awright, sir, Ah took mine!"

The next day the headmaster, after congratulating me on the great success of the previous evening, said to me that the local parish priest had pointed out to him that considerable sums must have accrued from the event. Typical of a parish priest to be so practical. The headmaster went on to say that he wished to help me and relieve me of as much anxiety as possible. He suggested that the best thing to do would be to put all the proceeds into the school funds and that he would pay from those funds any outstanding expenses. I thanked him for his well-meaning gesture of support but told him that, as this was a joint project, I would have to discuss the matter with the other members of the collective.

When I subsequently put the headmaster's proposition to them, and I did not fail to put it in its kindliest light, their response was curt, dismissive – and unanimous.

It was: "That'll be fucking right!"

When everything was 'divvied' or divided up, I was given an embarrassingly handsome share that allowed me to entertain my ill-deserving friends on the staff to a slap-up meal and drinks, plenty of them, at a local hostelry.

Reflecting on this experience gave me confidence about introducing cosmology into our timetable in the People's College. If the simple updated story of Noah and the Flood could produce such a ferment of intellectual enquiry and excitement in a bunch of school underachievers, so could the study of cosmology, if presented properly and appropriately, to my cohort of long-term unemployed people.

Some examples of how we went about doing this might not be amiss at this point.

TWELVE

In trying to convey the idea that they were not merely marginal onlookers or spectators of the cosmic drama, but rather at the very centre of it, I explained to them, for example, that if you created the fantasy of setting off on a journey from Craigmillar Crossroads and went in an unerringly straight line, you would cross over mountains and valleys, seas and rivers, cities and desert places and, so long as you never deviated from this imaginary straight line, because the earth is roughly round and because of gravity, you would come back unfailingly to your starting point at Craigmillar Crossroads. This is true whether you went north, south, east or west or any point in-between.

So, I would ask, "What does that tell you about Craigmillar?"

"That it's at the centre of the world," they would unhesitatingly reply.

"And what does that mean for you when you are standing at the crossroads in Craigmillar?"

"That I am the centre of the world."

"Not only the centre of the world," I would tell them, "but, because of the curvature of space, you are by the same token at the very centre of the whole cosmos."

One day, with another group of students, I varied the analogy, as one does as a teacher, and asked them, after the same build-up, what would happen if you fired a gun of almost infinite power straight ahead of you at Craigmillar Crossroads.

One wag in the class said, "Oh, I would never do that!"

"Why?" I asked.

"Because," he replied, "it would come right back roon and blow ma fuckin' heed aff!"

Of course, I had to tell them that if they were the centre of the world, so, by the same token, was every other human being on the planet. This in no way reduced them to insignificance. It simply meant that their undoubted power was a shared power.

On another occasion when we were considering how we came to exist and of what constituents we are made I began with this analogy (analogies were our stock in trade):

"Imagine," I said, "that you were asked to make a flag to symbolically represent a human being. The flag of Humanity, you might say. You could do worse than come up with a flag that is roughly in four quarters: one quarter would represent hydrogen, one oxygen, one nitrogen and one carbon."

Our bodies are mostly made up of water and that is two atoms of hydrogen to one of oxygen and all the other chemical elements in our bodies are represented by the two next in importance, that is, nitrogen and carbon, the building blocks of life.

All the hydrogen in the world was created in the first moment of the Big Bang. Therefore, through the hydrogen in our bodies we go back to the very beginnings of the universe. We carry the memory of that primal event captured in our own flesh and blood.

The generation of all the other elements, I would go on to explain, is the result of an event that is cosmically spectacular in its own right. It is called a Supernova.

When a star fifty or so times bigger than our own sun implodes and is destroyed, the light of the energy released is so colossal that it momentarily outshines in brightness all the billions of stars in its own galaxy. In its death throes the disintegrating star creates all the other elements in the periodic table. These elements, in the form of a gaseous mass, shoot off across space, coalesce with others on the way and ultimately congeal, as it were, to form star systems and planets like our own Solar System.

So, we can say that all of us were, in some sense, there at the beginning of time itself and have travelled halfway across the firmament to get here.

It is easy to see from all this that Earth is an intrinsic part of the cosmos as a whole.

At the subatomic level all the matter in the cosmos, including our own bodies, is made up of seething particles of energy which are governed by the same universal laws of quantum mechanics.

At the higher atomic or molecular level all the visible matter that we see in the universe (we will ignore for now the existence of invisible or dark matter because it is too problematic scientifically to serve our present purpose) has a common chemistry. Everything in the universe is composed of the same chemical elements that we find in the periodic table.

So, at the most fundamental level, we are part of the vast and seamless whole that is the fabric of the cosmos.

What happens at the smallest scales is replicated on the biggest scale of all, which is at the level of the large-scale structures of the cosmos, the stars, galaxies and planets without number in our universe. We are part of this massive network and participate in its remorselessly frantic activity.

When we look at the night sky on a clear night we see myriad pinpricks of light scattered across its surface. These pinpricks are nothing other than the light from stars and galaxies extremely remote from us in time and space (if these are not, in fact, the same thing). The sky appears to us as something fixed, unchanging and permanent. Yet this appearance of serenity and stillness in the heavens is only an illusion. In fact the whole cosmos and everything in it is in constant flux. As a result of the known explosive expansion of the cosmos, all the stars and galaxies are moving away from each other and from us here on Earth at incredible speeds.

So, if the universe is so turbulent and fast-moving, how come it appears to us as stationary and unchanging?

This has to do with the concept of motion and its relativity. When we are standing here on Earth looking idly at the scene before our eyes, we have no sense whatsoever of moving. Yet it is a startling fact that we on Earth are orbiting the sun at an incredible 67,000 miles an hour. At the same time the whole Solar System (the sun and its planets) are whizzing round the centre of our galaxy, the Milky Way, at an unbelievable 480,000 miles an hour!

The reason that we are moving at such colossal speeds and yet have no sensation of moving at all is that we lack any independent marker or frame of reference to show that we are moving.

It may help at this point if we compare two different modes of travel on Earth: a train travelling at speed through the countryside; and a jetliner flying at high altitude above the clouds.

In the case of the train we have a strong sense of moving fast because the trees and fields outside the window are flashing past us. These passing objects are our frame of reference. They tell us that we are moving.

There is no such frame of reference when we are travelling in the upper atmosphere in an aeroplane. So, we have no sense of moving at all.

How wise and prescient was the eighteenth century philosopher, George Berkeley, when he said, 'Without a frame of reference all motion is meaningless.'

The very first time I tried to convey these difficult and elusive concepts to my students in the People's College I ended that first course by saying to them: "Well, that is cosmology. What does it mean for you?"

One of the students, a single mother in her forties, I would guess, clasped her arms round her not insignificant bosom and said:

"Well, if ah get ye right, Paddy, it means that ah'm a star."

I ecstatically replied, "Right you are, Maggie. You are, literally and metaphorically, a star, for you are truly, in every sense, made out of the stuff of stars and walk among them like the Queen of Night."

THIRTEEN

What we studied in the People's College was not so much cosmology as applied cosmology. Not what cosmology is, in and of itself, but how it affects and enlightens us as individuals. How it makes sense in our own lives. How it impacts on our humanity.

In this respect my trainees and I were like weekend or recreational ice skaters. As such we did not require to know a hundred and one things about the complex physics and chemistry involved in the composition of the ice on which we skate. Strictly speaking, we needed to know only two big things, namely, that it would bear our weight and that it would have the critical degree of slipperiness to allow us to glide over its surface effortlessly. (Note that not all ice is slippery. In sub-zero temperatures, like in Alaska for example, it can have the surface consistency and intractability of sandpaper.)

Once these two minimal conditions are met, we are able to launch ourselves onto the ice and swoop around its curves in great swishing arcs of joy and liberation. Sometimes a certain degree of ignorance is bliss.

And bliss it was for us to set out on our little pilgrimage of knowledge, unburdened by useless and adipose facts and figures, but sustained by the stories we shared along the way and by our constant contemplation, via images and parables, if you like, of the ultimate purpose of our journey which was self-awareness.

That part of cosmology which concerns itself with chaos theory played an obvious part in this.

The Theory of Chaos tells us how quite diverse and, ultimately, vast effects can develop from exceedingly small starting points. The classic expression of this is what is called the Butterfly Effect. According to this effect the small perturbations or flapping of a butterfly's wings in Kansas can, after a long chain of miniscule events and increasingly amplified consequences, produce a hurricane much later in India.

In much the same manner this phenomenon can be seen at work in the present global warming crisis. Due to the rampant destruction of the carbon-capturing rainforests, when allied to the mass release into the atmosphere of carbon in the form of fossil fuels, till now locked up safely and harmlessly for millions of years in the bowels of the earth, we are changing and destabilising the planetary weather system – and we can see this happening before our very eyes every day.

The process of global warming that results from this exponential release of carbon is undoubtedly accelerating, due to the operation of the laws of chaos (if I might be permitted that oxymoron). Soon the effects will be worldwide and irreversible and will constitute a threat in no long time to the very existence of life on Earth by making the planet uninhabitable. And it is all our own fault; both the causing of it and the crass failure to respond to it. How true were the words of the great poet and mystic, Francis Thomson, when he said, 'Thou canst not stir a flower without troubling a star'!

An image I used a lot in this aspect of cosmology was the story of the snowflake. To a casual, and even not so casual, view all snowflakes look alike. And yet the startling fact is that no two snowflakes are, or can be, identical.

The shape of a snowflake is determined by its composition and state of origin and by its journey through the atmosphere. In this journey it is blown hither and thither randomly by the wind, collides with others, couples and decouples incessantly and is always at the mercy of sheer chance.

Only that particular snowflake has had that precise chaotic history. Of all the numberless snowflakes that there ever were, or will be, in the world's history no other snowflake could have that precise journey or fill that precise space. So, no two snowflakes could be exactly alike. However subtle or microscopic the differences in the journey might be, they would rule out the possibility of another snowflake having had that exact history, and, therefore, that exact shape. To have that exact shape it would have to be that snowflake.

Another analogy I used in this connection was what I called 'the empty desk'. I got them to imagine a time long ago in their lives, say when they were eight or nine years old. They set off from home that day to go for a walk.

They had no particular plan in starting off, no particular destination in mind. They were simply 'stravaiging', to use the couthy, old Scottish word.

When they reached the end of the road they could have gone either to the right or the left that day. It made absolutely no difference to them which way they went. Let's assume they went to the left. That decision set in motion a whole train of events – all small and unimportant in themselves – that led to them finishing up here a lifetime later in the People's College. If they had turned to the right that day I don't know where in the world – or out of it – they would have ended up. But one thing you can be sure of is that they would not have ended up here. In other words their desk would now be empty.

Two points need to be made at this juncture: firstly, there is no suggestion in this that our lives follow some predetermined, presumably divine, plan; secondly, it does not assume that our lives are dictated by pure, blind chance.

An important ingredient in all of this is the existence of consciousness. Our evolved – and constantly evolving – consciousness or awareness of self is part of the randomness and so affects the outcome, just like any other variable. This means that each moment in our lives is influenced by, yes, chance events, but also by our thinking response to them. We are, as thinking beings, not blind victims of fate, but in a real way participants in our destiny. In this way we are different to the snowflakes that can exercise absolutely no control over their fate.

It was by wilfully misunderstanding this concept that a friend of mine waggishly said, "When you drive through

Craigmillar you can always tell Pat's trainees. They're the ones standing rooted to the spot at Craigmillar Crossroads terrified to move to the right or the left for fear that their lives will take some horrible turn for the worse."

Of course, it could equally be said that my trainees and ex-trainees were characterised more positively – and more authentically – by their acquired existentialism, by their recognition that each moment in life is important and should be savoured and esteemed, because it is the womb of all future possibilities.

I break off at this juncture to relate a scrap of conversation between two trainees that I overheard one day through the open door to the kitchen. It is a not untypical example of how the trainees were struggling to accommodate themselves to some very difficult and even abstruse concepts.

"Tommy, how are you gettin' on wi' the cosmology course?"

"Well, tae tell you the truth, John, it's daein' ma heid in. Don't get me wrang, ah fair like aw thae wee stories Paddy tells us. You know, like how that wee butterfly sets aff a big storm in India. An' how there's nae two snowflakes the same. An' that empty desk idea. Ah can gist aboot get ma heid roon that. But this 'singyerauntie' stuff his got me right stumped an' no mistake. Ah cannae mak' heid nor tail of it."

"Singyerauntie? I don't get you, Tommy. Whit are ye on aboot?"

"That singyerauntie stuff. You know that wee tottie (tiny) thing that's no' the size o' tuppence and yet blows up intae the hale universe wi' hunners o' stars and planets."

"Oh, you mean Singularity! I get ye noo, Tommy. You mean that wee bit of something or nothing, as Paddy cries it, that is so small ye cannae see it and yet expands out fae an explosion, ca'ed the Big Bang, tae produce millions (no, hunners, by the way, Tommy, millions!) of stars and galaxies spread out o'er the whole of space."

"Aye, that's whit ah'm talkin' aboot. John, how can ye possibly explain that?"

"Well, it's no, easy. Ah'll gi'e ye that. The wey ah think o' it is this. It's like wan o' thae pop-up books that weans (children) get fur their Christmas. You know the kind o' thing ah mean. When you open the book, up springs, like magic, cardboard cut-outs of a wee village wi' trees and hooses an' people and maybes a wee dug walkin' aboot. Well, tae explain tae ye. When the book is shut, that's what went before the Big Bang – nothin'. Then, when you open it – that's the Big Bang – out comes the whole universe o' stars and planets that you couldnae count, even wi' a computer. Does that make sense tae ye, Tommy?"

"Aye, a bit. But what went before the Big Bang? That's whit ah'd like tae know. God, ah suppose?"

"Well that's what you and me think, Tommy, because we're baith Catholics. But, you see, maist o' the scientists don't believe in God so they cannae say that."

"Whit dae they say, then?" persisted Tommy.

"Well, Tommy, to tell the truth they hiv'nae got a clue. But that disnae stop them comin' up wi' some quare guesses – or theories, as they cry (call) them."

"Whit like, Johnny boy?"

"Well, wan o' their theories is that before oor pop-up book there was an even bigger pop-up book wi' a wee book as one of its pop-ups. This wee book, when you open it, is the one we've just been talkin' aboot that became oor universe. They call it 'the Baby Universes Theory.'"

"Fair enough. But whit went before that bigger book? An even bigger wan, I suppose?"

"I imagine that that's what they would have to say."

"Let me get this right. So, they're saying that there is a whole line of universes, aw wi' wee universes inside them, goin' back, whit? For ever? That disnae make any sense tae me. Ah think ah'll stick tae God, if you don't mind. But ah'll tell ye wan thing, John, see aw this stuff we're gettin' at the People's College, it sure makes you think, doesn't it?"

"Aye, that it does, Tommy, that it does. But that's what this college is aw aboot – making you think."

"Aye, Paddy fair likes the thinkin', doesn't he? And the writing."

"Aye, and the Celtic, Tommy, don't forget the Celtic."

I hope it will not be so difficult to see why cosmology, not only was included in our curriculum, but became a major factor in our success. It also brought us to the attention of a much wider world.

Serious professionals in the fields of employment and education from all over Europe, and, in one case, from as far away as Brazil, came to visit us and study our methods. We had interest in our work from two universities in France, one of them the Sorbonne. All were intrigued by the boldness of our inclusion of cosmology in a course of preparation for work and by our way of doing it. Interest from Scotland and England was disappointing to say the least, but this, modesty apart, says more, I feel, about the British than it says about my enterprise.

Predictably, in their chagrin, the council officials we dealt with went on disparagingly calling me 'The Star Man' behind my back. They just couldn't resist stoking up my ego.

FOURTEEN

Improving their qualifications and getting them psychologically ready for employment were the twin pillars of our programme of preparing our long-term unemployed trainees for the world of work. However, there remained the problem of actually getting a job. This would involve some hurdles that without our help the trainees would have difficulty surmounting. I am referring to the need to prepare a résumé or CV; to have some experience of interview technique; to acquire a good work ethic. These were people who in the main had never even seen a CV in their lives. Some had little or no experience of working and so we would have to prepare them for the culture shock of the workplace environment as well.

So, as it got towards the end of their college phase, we began to introduce elements of specific work-based training and preparation.

We started with the construction of a CV. We used no templates, consulted no books or manuals. We just sat down as a group to find a formula that answered all the needs of our trainees and would be well-received by employers. In this we were following the excellent advice of Blaise Pascal who said that 'we are generally better persuaded by the reasons we discover for ourselves than by those given to us by others'.

It should be said at this point that not all our trainees were unlettered and inadequate. Some, few, were even graduates. This applied in particular to our migrants.

We had at one period on our books two medical doctors from Bangladesh. They were husband and wife and in keeping with our rules of never having close relatives on our books at the same time, we took them on in successive intakes.

This arrangement proved useful for other unemployed married or unmarried couples too. It gave the family, not six months, but a whole year of security of income and yet with one parent always on hand to look after the family while the other was close by at the college. The continuity of income and its dependability gave them the opportunity to plan better as a family.

In addition it helped us to be seen not only as helping individuals but whole families. What with childcare and whole family involvement, there were always children coming in and out of our office. Than which, nothing was more welcome or more conducive to our core values.

The couple from Bangladesh were particularly interesting, because not only were they doctors, but they were both highly qualified surgeons with European postgraduate degrees in their field.

So, how, you will ask, did they end up in the People's College and on a scheme designed to assist the long-term unemployed?

Well, they qualified, like everyone else, by being registered unemployed. (Fatima's only job since arriving in Craigmillar had been working on the checkout of the local supermarket.) They would not be able to secure employment as doctors in any foreseeable future and, so, their unemployment was likely to be long-lasting.

This was due to the fact that, as a result of Cold War politics, their qualifications in Bangladesh were not recognised by the British Government. This was because they had acquired these qualifications at a university in Bangladesh during a two-year period when the UK Government for political reasons refused to recognise the new state of Bangladesh, formerly a part of Pakistan. Since they did not recognise the state it meant that they did not recognise its institutions, including its universities. As a result, the medical degrees of Mohammed and Fatima counted for nothing and they were not even allowed to present themselves for the examination that routinely permits doctors from a foreign jurisdiction to qualify to practise medicine in the United Kingdom. They were stuck in a trap from which there seemed to be no escape.

So, why did they insist on coming to Britain, where they would not be able to pursue their profession, when they could have done so almost anywhere else in the world, except the equally recalcitrant United States? Well, the simple answer to that is, I just don't know. And I never got to know either. For whatever reason, they were both drawn obsessively to Britain and nothing else would do.

Though I never saw the need to probe their reasons for this decision, I suspect that it had something to do with the Raj mentality.

They had grown up in a British colony, subject to the Raj and its culture. Fatima was the daughter of an Indian sergeant-major in the British Army. He had an abounding love of Britain and the British Crown and even felt himself British in some sense, though I am sure he was never encouraged in this delusion by his British masters. He brought up his family of six girls, all of whom graduated from university, to respect, to the point of veneration, the British Crown and its institutions. I don't know so well the family history of her husband, Mohammed, but it must have been similar or else the attractions of Fatima must have proved overwhelmingly decisive.

In any event, here they were, undoubtedly unemployed, and migrants to boot: what else could I do but take them on? Of course, I know what you are thinking. What kind of job could I get for them? How could two such highly qualified and educated people benefit from the rather basic education we were offering?

The answer to these questions will be revealed later in the story and I can promise it will surprise you.

As will the story of another graduate of ours, a Nigerian woman, who had fled her country after a military coup. She had been a successful teacher for many years in Nigeria. By fleeing the country she had so angered the new regime that they refused to divulge, and, therefore, authenticate, her qualifications or her experience as a teacher. Without this authentication she would never be able to resume her profession in Britain. So, though for different reasons, her predicament was similar to that of Mohammed and Fatima. She was caught in a political net from which there appeared no possibility of escape.

What we managed to do for this woman is no less interesting, though arguably more dramatic, than we were able to do for Mohammed and Fatima and will also be revealed later in this story.

These were not the only graduates who came on to our books over the years, though graduates were always naturally a tiny minority in the context of our usual population. All were victims of fate in one respect or another and all found a home with us and a future.

Other surprising minority cases that appear in our story include a businessman whose business had collapsed some time before under a mountain of debt and amid suspicions of fraud and a successful professional footballer whose career had ended prematurely due to his addiction to gambling and alcohol. Both these people had enjoyed great success in life – and wealth – before falling on hard times and finally ending up in poverty-stricken Craigmillar.

Neither of them had any reason to regret their decision to join their classmates in the People's College, as you will discover for yourself later in the story.

FIFTEEN

The CV structure we came up with had four sections: all were rather obvious, but we found our way to them by our own journey and that was the most important thing.

The first section we called PERSONAL DETAILS and contained basic information, like name, address, age and telephone number.

The only real problem we encountered in this section was whether to include Craigmillar in the address. Obviously, it would be usual to write, for example,

19 Something Avenue,

Craigmillar, Edinburgh

But, of course, this caused a problem because of the unsavoury reputation of the Craigmillar Estate at that time. Some suggested simply deleting the word 'Craigmillar' from the address, for, as one student put it, "These people oot there think that folk frae Craigmillar are nuthin' but a bunch o' bams." However, this simple, but swingeing, solution would present difficulties at the central sorting office for it would assume that every individual sorter would have a very good, even intimate, knowledge of all the individual streets in Edinburgh – and this could not be guaranteed. These were the days before postal codes.

The irony of this situation was that in medieval times Craigmillar had been a very desirable address. Craigmillar boasts to this day a famous castle, one of the best preserved in Scotland, that played, at times, an important role in the history of Scotland. Craigmillar Castle was said to have been Mary, Queen of Scots' favourite castle and the lands around it had been a highly prized hunting ground of the Stuart kings for centuries.

It is also the place where, it is claimed, the murder of David Rizzio, the court musician and favourite of Mary, Queen of Scots, was planned by factions of the notoriously disloyal Scottish nobility.

So, at least it could be said that its later reputation for violence in the period that concerns us at the moment is nothing new.

In the end we left it up to each individual to decide for themselves whether to keep 'Craigmillar' in or leave it out. Understandably, the majority followed that old piece of timeless wisdom, 'When in doubt, leave it out.'

The second section and the third suggested themselves.

The second section dealt with previous educational experience under the headings:

SCHOOL/COLLEGE   DATES   QUALIFICATIONS

For most of our students the only thing that they could put into the qualifications section was the certificates they received from the People's College itself. This was the first fruit of our education-based programme. It is easy to imagine their pride when they listed their qualifications in English, Mathematics, Modern Studies and Spanish in this section of the CV. It was quite a handful for a bunch of school failures. It signalled to the world that they were proceeding at full sail and, crucially, now under their own colours.

The main problems occurred with the next section which we called:

EMPLOYMENT HISTORY

Almost everyone, except the ensainted, has some dodgy bits in this portion of their CV. Bits they have to get round or play down in some way. For our trainees the dodgy bits far outweighed the others. These problem areas or discontinuities in work history were due to a number of factors, such as sackings, personal or domestic crises, imprisonment or illness. In some cases major work was going to have to be done to construct a CV that would not be rejected out of hand.

The first, and absolutely binding, requirement, as I warned them, was that in the CV they should not tell any lies. No outright lies, that is. There is nothing wrong with stretching the truth. We managed to get rid of some, less than a year, incidents of unemployment by the simple expedient of only using years, rather than months and years, when recording periods of employment. Of course, this is a form of lying, lying by omission, but we were comfortable with the fact that by this subterfuge we did not commit ourselves to an outright falsehood. It is, after all, a fairly normal practice in society at large; in politics it is called spin and in business advertising. It comes under the heading of being economical with the truth and this is widely perceived in society at large as being acceptable and even laudable.

We employed the same sort of astuteness in describing the jobs they had in the past to make them seem as impressive and responsible as possible. I remember one conversation I had with one of our female trainees. She had left school at fifteen to join a well-known furrier's firm in Glasgow. She had worked there for a number of years in a series of jobs of no great merit. I knew that the firm in question had gone out of business some time ago, so I felt freer in our search for a more impressive way of describing her work there.

I asked her, "Bridget, when you were working in that firm what happened at five o'clock when the hooter sounded?"

She answered, "We finished our—"

I stopped her right there.

"That's right. You finished. And you worked in fur. So you could say, could you not, that you were a fur finisher?"

This is what we put down for her under the heading of TYPE OF WORK, Fur Finisher. It was, after all, a harmless piece of craftiness and involved no hurt to anyone and was really not all that different from the truth. By giving Bridget a job title that implied some degree of specialisation we were merely giving her a little extra lustre in the eyes of the reader of her CV that would be denied her if she were to describe herself, with more fiddling accuracy, as a simple assembly-line worker. It is a technique the Jesuits call 'occult compensation' (if someone steals your cow and you have no legal means of recovering it, then, according to the Jesuits, you commit no sin by stealing it back from them).

Years ago there was a very popular comedian, by the name of Frank Carson, who had the catchphrase, 'It's the wey ah tell them!'. In life in general, it is all about the way you tell it. My mother used to say, "Never say a bad word about yourself." She knew that if you said anything derogatory about yourself, even in jest, it acquired much greater veracity and could come back to hurt you much more than something said about you by another. After all, at least the latter can be denied.

So our technique in this section of the CV could be described not as misleading people but as refusing to say anything detrimental. So, we simply avoided saying anything that would be discreditable to them or, more usually, skated round it as gracefully and astutely as possible.

So, having covered PERSONAL DETAILS, EDUCATIONAL EXPERIENCE and EMPLOYMENT HISTORY it only remains useful to the employer to say something about yourself, your personality, the human being behind the facts. We regarded this as the most vital and illuminating part of the CV. This was the part of the CV where they 'sold' themselves to an employer, allowed their name to jump out of the bunch. We called this section, naturally enough, PERSONAL SKILLS AND INTERESTS.

Through discussion we encouraged our trainees to make an inventory of those personal skills or interests they had that made them that little bit different to everyone else. It could be an ability like dancing, swimming or playing football or an interest like pigeon fancying, card collecting or ballroom dancing. Anything that allows their particular personality to reveal itself.

I was convinced that this was the most important section of the CV because it gave the potential employer the opportunity to see the actual person behind the screen of dates and facts.

This reminds me of an incident that took place in my early years at the People's College when I was starting to make my reputation there. A group of teachers from the local high school invited me to give a talk about my work in the People's College to their pupils. I was happy to do so and flattered, I suppose.

However, unknown to me, it was an elaborate trap to have some fun at my expense. As classroom teachers they had a great antipathy to advisors generally and were very well aware of my having been one. Advisors were held in contempt by many teachers because they were sufficiently far enough above them on the hierarchical educational ladder to constitute part of the hated establishment and yet, as teachers themselves, were close enough to inspire envy at their success.

That it was a set-up only occurred to me when I turned up at the school and discovered that my audience was not to be a small group of near-leaving seniors but the whole of the second year. Second year pupils are notoriously difficult to handle. They are over their first-year nervousness at being at the big school and their hormones are at their most uncontrollable peak.

I realised that I was being sent into the arena to face wild beasts. This was reinforced by the fact that all six or seven teachers, Mme Defarges to a man and woman, instead of taking a welcome break as would have been normal in the circumstances, decided to stay and witness the bloody mauling of a hated advisor. I had not the slightest doubt that this was the inescapable fate that awaited me, particularly when they asked me not to just talk about my work but 'to put the fear of death in them about the evils of unemployment'!

However, my mother did not raise any stupid children and I had no intention of speaking about unemployment or its evils, especially to that young audience. Instead, I began by saying to them, "These people here (pointing dismissively at the teachers who ringed the room) have asked me to talk to you about unemployment but that is just daft. You have no interest, nor should you have at your age, in the matter of employment. This would be a complete waste of your time and mine. Instead of me speaking to you about things that I know about and you don't, which is what teachers are always doing, I want you to tell me about things that you know that I don't have a clue about – and neither, by the way, do these people standing against the wall. Let's talk about your skills.

"First of all, let me ask you a question. If I fell down right now in front of you with a heart attack, how many of you would know what to do?"

Four hands went up, rather hesitantly.

"Alright, you," I said, pointing to a girl near the front.

She began to talk, nervously at first but growing in confidence when she realised that everyone in the room was listening attentively. She talked about ensuring that I was in the right position and comfortable and went on to describe the procedures involved in CPR.

After her excellent contribution she was warmly applauded by the whole group and resumed her seat with an air of satisfaction.

Then I went on to say, "Look, I know nothing about fishing and I am sure your teachers haven't a clue about it either (I clearly implied that there were a great number of things they knew nothing about). Yet I am fascinated by it. Who can persuade me that I should take up fishing?"

About fifteen hands were raised, quite enthusiastically this time. One tough-looking boy began the discussion but very quickly it was a conversation in which all the participants were vying with each other to offer ideas, make corrections or just generally enjoy themselves talking about something they liked and that mattered to them.

The chagrin of the teachers round the room was visible to all and very pleasing, not only to me but also to the pupils themselves, who nurtured their own private animosities against them and were enjoying their discomfiture.

And it got better, as I proposed subject after subject: pigeon-keeping, the female arts of knitting and crocheting, Irish dancing (accompanied by many a lively and hilarious demonstration), street games and other urban diversions. The pupils tumbled over themselves to have their moment in the sun. The room was filled with laughter and good-humoured rivalry. So much so that when the bell rang to end the session it came as a surprise to everyone and was greeted by an audible moan of disappointment from the pupils.

At this point the teachers, driven mad that their plot to destroy me had backfired and reverting to type, leapt forward like dervishes and screamed at the group, "Don't move a muscle! Not a muscle! Stay in your places!"

In fact, no one in the whole year group had made any kind of move to leave. So, I decided to impose myself on the situation by saying to the teachers, "Butt out! We have not needed your help before and we sure as hell don't need it now!"

This got a huge cheer from the pupils (no doubt the mild expletive helped) who on my signal began to leave the hall in a very orderly manner. The chastened teachers took advantage of this silent exodus to mingle with the crowd and fade away.

Getting back to the present; of course, not all the skills that my trainees had were equally acceptable. Some were irrelevant or would give a poor impression of their lifestyle. So, we conceived the theory of 'pictures in the mind'. When some skill or interest was mentioned I would ask the trainees what picture it might conjure up in the mind of a potential employer.

For example, if someone said they liked playing pool, it was agreed that this conveyed the image or picture of a dingy, smoke-filled basement where people were lounging about fecklessly, or even feloniously, while playing their boringly repetitive games of unremarkable pool. So, better keep that to ourselves.

On the other hand, if you were the champion of your local snooker club or a finalist at a higher level that would be good. This presented the picture of someone constantly practising to reach a high level of skill and having the requisite determination to succeed. Naturally, exhibiting determination to succeed as well as competency are very potent attractors for an employer.

But there are other, less tangible but very important, assets, like, for example, being fit and healthy, being a good team player or being trustworthy with goods or information. We found that the best way of indicating these more tenuous qualities was not by stating them baldly. That could be counterproductive. Someone once said – I forget who – that if a person, seeking entrance to your house for some reason were to take the trouble to assure you that they were honest, you would be well advised to count the spoons.

We decided that the best way to convey these virtuous elements is obliquely, by demonstration, by putting the appropriate picture in the mind of the reader. The best way to convey that you are healthy and active is by making reference to some specific activity or interest that would imply good health, such as, for example, swimming, climbing, running, or, even, walking.

Walking was the great get-out-of-jail card in the matter of physical activities – for everyone, except, God help them, the disabled, can walk. In the absence of any other physical recreation for which you could claim credit you could always say that you enjoyed walking. No one could gainsay or question that simple and common activity. All it needed for full effectiveness was the addition of a subtle element of specificity. Thus, instead of saying you liked walking, you could say that you had a love of hillwalking, or taking forest walks, or strolling along some (named and well-known) beach. This made it seem somehow more focused, and, therefore, more significant and impressive. Such petty tricks and stratagems were meat and drink to my little community in the People's College whose main tool for survival from infancy had been living by their wits.

We decided, furthermore, that the section on Skills and Interests should ideally include, a) something that suggests fitness or health, b) something that suggests at least mild intellectuality, like reading, doing crosswords, playing chess and c) something that suggests congeniality or public-spiritedness, like being in a club or some sort of an association or being part of a campaign. Of course, having all three would be nice but two out of three would be sufficient, we felt.

And so, the day finally arrives when our trainees, having completed their studies and armed with their qualifications and a CV that well reflects their abilities and aptitudes, stand on the threshold of a new life. No longer the shambling, insecure individuals who presented themselves at our door in the first place, they are now, almost without exception, dynamic, confident and ambitious free spirits ready to engage with the world on their own terms.

They have, however, one last bridge to cross – the dreaded interview – which will, inevitably, face them in whatever direction they choose to go or life takes them. Submitting themselves to outside examination is the final test of their progress to date and is the door that opens out to a bright future of self-sufficiency and dignity in employment.

SIXTEEN

Of course, not all of our trainees would strictly require a CV to obtain a job.

Most of the men were looking for jobs of a manual nature. For such jobs a CV was not a normal expectation. They were expected only to demonstrate their fitness for the work through a more or less exhaustive interview. Such interviews would normally take place between individuals, interviewer and interviewee, with a shared linguistic register and common social perspectives and, so, would not prove particularly difficult. Certainly not, for the robust, articulate and confident individuals we were producing in the People's College.

For most of the male trainees the normal route into employment was the experience we gained for them through their placement. Even where a job did not materialise with the placement employer, the experience gained through it had great value to other employers, particularly in terms of the work ethic displayed and the recommendation that went with it.

Some of the younger ones managed to get apprenticeship positions and this represented a big success for us. Of course, this was before the great reduction in apprenticeships during the Thatcher years which was part of the Tory Government's strategy of replacing skilled, well-trained and, crucially, well-organised workers with biddable amateurs who 'could do the job'. This led directly to the creation of the unregulated 'cowboy culture' in the building trade that is the bane of so many householders to this day.

Sometimes our influence on their entry into work came through contacts. This was especially true of jobs gained with the Edinburgh Council. One trainee, and I have always felt that this was one of our greatest successes, managed to get a job as a Council binman.

Charlie was almost illiterate when he came to us and was shy beyond description. He had a bad stutter and this had leached away all his confidence in his ability to secure employment. Nevertheless, he had his heart set on getting a job as a Council binman. The job was well paid and would be well within his capabilities, since it did not call for significant spoken or written skills.

The drawback with this job was that the sector was wracked by a particular form of nepotism according to which these coveted jobs passed mainly from father to son or through family or friendship connections. When we managed to find him a placement with the Council's Refuse Department, through our own connections, he was delighted (in his phrase, 'over the moon').

The memory of the excited and happy expression on

his face the day he told us that he had got the job with the council will remain with me forever.

We never felt that any job, however elevated on the social scale, is, inherently, any better than another. All work has its own dignity and integrity and it was central to our philosophy that we sought to find the best match for our trainees in terms of their abilities and their aspirations. So, Charlie was, and always will be to us, an authentic star and one of our most pleasing outcomes.

I cannot fail to recall at this juncture an interview I once saw on television involving Muhammed Ali, arguably the greatest heavyweight boxer of all time.

In answer to the question, "What would have become of you, if you hadn't been a boxer?" he said that he would have been great no matter what he had taken up. As he put it, "If I had been a garbage collector, I would have been the best garbage collector in the world."

Better even than Charlie, then?

For the majority of our trainees a good CV would be a primary requirement and developing a good interview technique a priority.

The prospect of the interview frightened and unsettled most of our trainees who, for one reason or another, had mostly negative experience of their dealings with figures in authority. Not always through any fault of their own.

We needed to build up their confidence and boost their feelings of self-worth. They had to lose all sense of inferiority and go into the interview as if it were a boxing match where they had, at least, a fighting chance. How they responded to these macho images!

It was our job to adjust the odds in their favour. We did this, of course, in a general way by everything that the People's College did for them and by the values we stood for. But we did it specifically by putting them at the centre of everything. We drummed into them that the interview itself would be conducted on their terms, on the basis of the CV that they had prepared. They were in charge of what went into the document and, so, were able, in an important sense, to dictate how the conversation would develop.

The first essential, we told them, was that they must know their CV inside out and be able to respond to any question arising from it with confidence and ease. This would require effort on their part to internalise all the information on the CV and anticipate any problematic moments, having ready a well-considered response.

It would require practice and rehearsal. This was something in which we had a very strong faith. We rehearsed everything – even how to walk into a room. I had read somewhere that most interviews are decided in the first ninety seconds. I don't know where I came upon this piece of information but it seemed entirely plausible because it matched my own experience of life which told me that first impressions are often critical. If there was any truth in this statement, then it meant that the interviewee had barely time to come in the door, walk a few steps to the seat prepared for them and say their name before the magic ninety seconds were up and with them possibly their chance of a job.

So, we got our trainees, one after another, to practise walking into the room, taking a seat and then saying their name.

It is surprising how many different ways there are of doing such a simple thing. The other trainees, now the judging panel, would appraise them – and they did so ruthlessly and insightfully. Criticisms like "you looked scared shitless", "you shoogled (moved provocatively) yer arse o'er much", "you looked as if ye wur goin' tae bash his heed in", filled the room and were taken on board for future attempts.

We rehearsed everything, even how to sit in the chair. Do you sit in it comfortably, using its full depth? Or do you sit upright on the front edge of it as if ready to leap into action? Some people, when taking a seat, have the habit, especially if nervous, of instinctively pulling it forward a little. The class decided that this was a bad idea because moving yourself closer to the interviewer, invading his space as it were, could come across as an aggressive or threatening act. At the very least it implied that the interviewer had not put the seat in the right place to begin with.

Often there were no wrong or right answers: it all depended on the personality of the person being interviewed, what he or she felt comfortable with. Sometimes, paradoxically, we had to rehearse out of them the comfortable or instinctive response. For example, we had to persuade some of them, when faced with a particularly difficult or problematic question, to resist giving the habitual, but terribly revealing, response of, 'no comment'.

Naturally, rehearsing how to come into a room and sit down is only part of the interview technique that they would have to acquire. There was the interview itself.

We organised mock interviews with someone playing the part of the inquisitorial interviewer and the interviewees, one after another, having to pit their wits against them. Obviously, the roles rotated, but they were always lively, hard-hitting and fun-filled occasions.

This became even more the case when we had visitors from outside taking part in the role-playing. I was lucky enough to know personally a number of prominent personalities in the world of Scottish theatre and television. Thus, regular visitors to the People's College included famous actors, such as Andy Gray, Elaine C Smith and Bill Paterson. You can easily imagine how excited our trainees were to be improvising mock interviews with people they had only ever seen on television.

I vividly remember one mock interview in which Andy Gray, the great Scottish comic actor, was playing the interviewer.

In a pseudo-posh English accent, he asked the trainee he was interviewing, "I see from your CV, my good man, that you claim to have management experience. Forgive me if I rather doubt that. Would you care to expand on that statement? Perhaps explain how it came about?"

The interviewee, who had only recently been released from prison after serving a sentence of twelve years for GBH (Grievous Bodily Harm), answered somewhat tartly, "While ah wis serving my time in Peterhead Prison, ah personally organised and managed the longest-running rooftop protest in the history of the British Prison Service. For three lang weeks, some of the toughest villains of Scottish crime faced up to the ferocious attacks of hunners of well-armed and ruthless prison officers and police and got oursels a stalemate. Now, ah don't whit you mean by management but that took some managin', ah can tell you!"

The actor took the unintentional rebuff in very good part and laughed as much as anyone in the class at the manner in which he had been bested in the exchange.

And so, by hook and by crook, through laughter and tears, we got them ready to face up to the world of work, armed with CVs they knew backwards and the experience gained from the mock interviews. Like thoroughly well-prepared athletes, they were poised and ready to take the next step which was into employment.

Before dealing with the employment outcomes gained for our trainees, there is one element of our work which has not already been covered and which deserves major attention. I refer to the need to resolve some criminal issues that hung over many of our population from their previous life as offenders. I will deal later with this critical aspect of our work but first I must outline some of the more generalised and basic problems that confronted all of our trainees.

SEVENTEEN

The main priority of our European Social Funded scheme was to provide permanent jobs for the long-term unemployed people of this very deprived area and thus reduce the unemployment statistics in one of the most deprived areas in Europe. This is why we were able to take on to our scheme only people that were on the official register, or books, of the Labour Exchange Bureau, or the Broo as it was called locally.

These were people who were in receipt of unemployment benefit and one function of the initiative was, therefore, to reduce the national benefit bill. This obligation wasn't difficult to comply with, for the people of Craigmillar weren't daft. If they were not earning money they would be claiming benefit. It did, however, give us one particular problem which I will deal with later.

The other expectation of the funding was that we should target the particularly vulnerable, ex-drug addicts, ex-alcoholics, ex-criminal offenders and single mothers. We did adhere to this condition scrupulously but, oddly, our funders never once required of us documentary evidence for these categories of special need. They simply took our word for it. And well they might, because in Craigmillar at that time it would have been difficult to find anyone who did not have problems with drink, drugs, criminality or family breakdown. Sometimes these categories overlapped each other. We even had, exceptionally, trainees that covered all four categories.

The only iron rule was that they should be ex-whatever-they-were and in all of my thirteen years in the People's College I never knew a single example of someone turning up at our unit affected by drink or drugs. This was one of the little miracles of our enterprise. We kept them busy and motivated and they for their part were determined to seize what was, most likely, their last chance to put their lives back together again.

Undoubtedly the fact that we were able to pay them an allowance, which we insisted on calling a wage, was a big factor in this. It meant that they were officially off benefit and virtually, as it were, already in work, at least as far as the social security system was concerned. This was a very important consideration for their motivation and personal sense of worth.

Furthermore we had the great good fortune that we were able to provide full childcare.

Obviously this was a necessity for our single mothers but it was available to any single parent and had the effect of giving them, when combined with their 'wage', the equivalent of a decent income. This became later a stick for our back because it meant that the jobs we found for them had to pay at least the equivalent of salary and childcare costs combined. This had the effect of just making us set our sights higher when finding them work. It never proved an insuperable obstacle.

That said, it did represent an embarrassment to us on one particular occasion.

We had arranged a placement for two of our female trainees with a business in the seaside resort of Portobello in the southside of Edinburgh. This business was a co-operative venture set up by some enterprising young women of the area and involved a cafe that dealt exclusively with ethically produced ingredients in a robust artisan style.

There was a basic social mismatch between the proprietors of this business, who were middle-class vegetarians, and our unsophisticated carnivores. However, this did not in itself cause any problems and the relations between the greatly disparate parties were, on the whole, excellent. No, what caused the placements to fall apart was that oldest and most insidious of all human defects – the green-eyed monster, Jealousy.

These smart and sophisticated young businesswomen couldn't bear it when they discovered that our trainees, with the wage we paid them and the free childcare that we provided, were better off than they were!

Because they were at that stage building up a business from nothing, they were able to pay themselves only a small wage. At the same time they were having to pay childcare costs for their own children out of this paltry income. They could not but be resentful of the fact that because of this they, the proprietors of the business, were effectively less well off than their 'employees' from the nearby housing estate of Craigmillar.

For all the help our nil-cost trainees were to them in building up the business, they, in the end, could not bear the perceived shame of it and asked us to terminate the placements. There was no rancour or animosity on either side at this mutual parting of the ways. I only hope that they did not live to regret their pusillanimity.

As for us, we just picked ourselves up, dusted ourselves down and moved on. As was our way, when one door closed we simply knocked on all the other doors in sight till another one opened for us. One almost always did.

EIGHTEEN

It goes without saying that people with the range and depth of personal problems that I have outlined do not get over them easily. So how did we help them to adjust to normal life? We did this by providing a welcoming, non-judgemental atmosphere in the college. We never confronted their problems openly or directly, either at the individual or the group level. We left matters like health and societal rehabilitation to the professionals in the medical and probationary services.

You would have thought that with my own experience of alcoholism I would have been able to prove helpful to those trying to get off the drink. Well, in a very general way I was. I never hid from them my previous problems with alcohol and told them stories of my previous addiction designed to encourage them in their own struggles.

I remember telling them of one incident I was involved in when I was attending a European Social Fund function in Dublin. This event took the form of a lavish dinner and the principal guest was the President of Ireland, at that time Mary Robinson. We were all seated at long tables and I found myself sitting opposite a delightful little nun, in her seventies I would guess.

At one point a circulating bottle of wine was passed to me. Without comment I passed it on to my next in line. Not long afterwards, this, or more likely a bottle like it, was handed to me by the dining companion on my immediate right. Once again I declined, but this time my fellow guest, who had noticed my first refusal, said, "Come on, Pat, get into it! Don't be shy. Sure, you're in Dublin and it's on the house. Get your neck round it!"

I explained to him that I used to drink but that I had given it up some time ago. With a mumbled "fair play to you" he resumed his former conversation.

A little while later the elderly nun, who had the most marvellously twinkling eyes you ever saw, leaned towards me and said, "Pat, you said you used to drink but gave it up. Can I ask you? How did you manage it? What did you do about it?"

I said, "I did the only thing that an alcoholic can – and should – do, Sister. I joined Alcoholics Anonymous."

Later in the evening, after the dinner and an address from the President of Ireland, we were all milling about talking, as one does at the close of a conference. Out of the blue the little nun appeared at my elbow and asked if she could have a word with me in private. We adjourned to a quiet corner of the great hall where we would be undisturbed. Once there, she looked me straight in the eye and said, "So you tell me that you're in t'AA."

I said, "Yes, I am, Sister."

At once her hand shot out from the sleeve of her habit and she said, "Then, shake, for so am I!"

She went on to confide in me that she only ever drank on her own in her room at night and then only the hard stuff (she glanced dismissively in the direction of the wine bottles still visible on the tables behind us). She went on to explain that she had got away with her secret drinking for years until one morning the Mother Superior said to her, "Eileen, what in the name of God is going on? Sure, the sisters can't get a wink of sleep for you singing 'Killarney' at three-thirty in the morning."

She invited me to go with her to her AA meeting that night at Findlayson's Church just off O'Connell Street. I was more than happy to accept her invitation.

It proved to be an unforgettable experience. The sharers were extremely eloquent and funny. You would have paid money to listen to them. Particularly an old sea captain who had us in stitches with tales of his drinking exploits on the ocean wave.

I can't help reflecting at this point on the many meetings of AA I have attended over the years. They tend to split into two main groups. There are sharings, often scathingly referred to as drunkalogs, in which harrowing tales are told of all the evils and troubles that drink brought into their lives. Tales of marriage breakdowns, family estrangements, lock-up wards, blackouts and humiliations in abundance. Other meetings, like the one in Findlayson's Church, are more light-hearted in tone and can even be hilarious at times. This is not so surprising, as these are often the very same people who were once the life and soul of the party. In sobriety they are still the same people with the same zest for telling a story.

Of course, there is a place for both approaches in AA. Too much of one or the other could prove unpalatable and, therefore, unhelpful to certain people and could threaten their sobriety.

However you look at it, the business of staying sober is a serious matter. The great quality of AA is that you are enjoined to listen to people's stories without judging them and take from them what is useful to ensure your continued sobriety. To achieve this two things must happen: that particular person must be there to tell their story; and you must be there to hear it.

This hit home to me on one particular occasion.

It had come to my attention that someone from my past was trying to cause problems for me that were potentially damaging to my ability to secure a particular job. It was a job that meant a great deal to me at the time. I flew into a rage such as I had seldom experienced before at the injustice of it and the malice behind it. I raved against the man and swore that I would kill him if I could get my hands on him. My rage was so extreme that I knew instinctively that it was a threat to my sobriety and that, therefore, I had to get to an AA meeting.

So off I went, cursing the while, to my regular Coburn Street meeting place in the middle of Edinburgh. I reached the door and was just about to press the entry bell when I realised that if I went in there, they would take my anger away – and I didn't want that! So I walked away. I returned to the door once again and once again I couldn't ring the bell. Then I came back the third time and this time I did ring the bell and joined the meeting.

The really serious work in an AA meeting comes when the members share their experience, their problems and sometimes their little triumphs. As with everything in AA, the sharing is voluntary; you can choose to just sit and listen if you like. But that night I wanted to speak – and how! Although you are expected to speak only in generalities, my rage manifested itself clearly enough. When it came his turn to speak, a young man across the room from me who seemed, in appearance and culture, as far as you could get from me – we would never have bumped into each other in life except at an AA meeting – said simply that he wanted to talk to me in private after the meeting.

When we met up later he said to me, "You are in a bad way, pal. I heard you say that you could kill this guy. And I believe you. I think you would be perfectly capable of doing so. I know this because I was released just this morning from prison in Glasgow after serving five years for manslaughter and, let me tell you, I wasn't half as angry with the man I killed as you are now. You are in real danger, pal."

Then, changing tack, he asked me, "See this guy that is causing you all this grief, what is he doing right now?"

Still angry I said, "How the fuck do I know?!"

He said, patiently, "Humour me. Just take a guess. Is he running about like a dafty, banging his head against the walls in rage at you? Or is he sitting quietly at home having a glass of wine with his wife?"

Grudgingly I admitted that it was probably the latter.

"Exactly!" said he. "So who's the eejit (idiot) here? You can end it all just by letting it go. I remember an old cellmate of mine, who had spent most of his life in jail, once telling me in a similar situation, 'The snake can bite you once – or, if you're really unlucky, even twice – but always remember that it has to live its whole life with its venom.' So my advice to you is to just walk away, forget it. Let him keep his venom. You spit it out and you're rid of it – and him. Forever!"

His words hit me like a hammer blow. After leaving him, I had only walked about fifty yards up the road when, as if by magic, my anger left me, never to return. If I had happened to bump into my enemy at that moment, I don't say that I would have shaken him by the hand but I would have nodded a hello.

For AA to work its magic my unknown friend, who was the only one in the world that could have helped me in that way at that time had to turn up at that particular meeting (he admitted that he did not know what possessed him to go to Edinburgh that night) and I had to make myself available to his help by ringing that bell.

NINETEEN

Chance played a great part in our recruitment process. We had no control over who came to our door or the reasons why they did so. But we did not automatically accept everyone. Because of the need for solidarity and mutual respect, the people we recruited would have to be able to work together in some kind of harmony. One bad apple could have had devastating consequences for the success of our highly delicate operation.

In this respect the contribution of our secretary, Lizzie Harkins, was critical. Lizzie was a delightfully bubbly person, highly skilled in all aspects of the clerical work involved. However, her real value to us was her vast knowledge of the local area and its people. She was able to spot, and allow us to root out, any potential toe-rag that could threaten the delicate balance of our group. She did this fearlessly, for she was a very spunky and determined woman.

From the first, we had no end of candidates who applied to join the VTU, not least because of the financial incentive that it offered. Having Lizzie on the premises meant that we were less vulnerable to those that wished to join us for purely financial reasons and were more aware of those with special need of our help, such as the particularly vulnerable set of people we were bound to target.

Additionally, Lizzie was able to protect us, through her intimate local knowledge, from problems that arose in the operation of our scheme. Take, for example, the real possibility that some trainees could involve themselves in fraud by remaining on unemployment benefit while in receipt of our 'wage'. This was a grave worry for us which could have had serious consequences for the perpetrators, as well as for ourselves in the long run.

On one occasion when I had some suspicion that this type of fraud might be happening I phoned the Labour Exchange to ask if such and such a person was in receipt of benefit. They refused to divulge this information on the grounds of privacy. Even when I explained who I was and that my request was driven by my desire to prevent someone getting themselves into trouble, as well as thwarting a fraud against the state, they remained adamant.

Fortunately, Lizzie came, as usual, to our assistance. She just seemed to know who was in receipt of benefit and who wasn't. Her effectiveness in this stewardship is vouched for by the fact that no example of this type of fraud was ever uncovered in the whole thirteen years of the existence of our unit.

Mind you, we came close to it at times and had to be eternally vigilant.

I remember one such occasion vividly. One of our trainees was in the second phase of his training and was in placement with a firm of builders. I had reason to believe, but could not be certain, that he was still 'signing on'. (Turning up once a week at the Labour Exchange to confirm with a signature that you were still unemployed, but available for work, was a condition of receiving state benefit.) This meant that he would have been receiving double benefit all through the period of his training; our 'wage' and the requisite unemployment allowance. It was, therefore, a situation with potentially very serious consequences for him and for us, reputationally.

I racked my brains to come up with a solution which would be as harmless as possible for all. I was loath to simply dismiss him from our books. This would have exposed our seeming negligence and, more importantly, would have prevented us from having the opportunity to preserve our excellent statistics which were based on getting trainees into employment.

Since nothing had yet been discovered officially about this possible fraud, my first necessity was to get him off our books before anything dire happened. But how to protect our exit statistics? Then I had a brainwave. But would it work?

I called him into my office and said to him, "Frankie, do you have something to tell me?"

"No, Paddy," he said innocently, for he had no idea about my suspicions.

"Listen, Frankie, you know I am always on your side and wish only to keep you out of trouble. I have had the

Fraud Squad on to me asking about you (this was a lie). I have held them off but they're getting back to me tomorrow morning and I will have to answer their questions honestly. So, tell me, have you been signing on?"

He was almost reduced to tears with shame and worry.

"Ah'm really sorry, Paddy. Ah hiv' been signing on. Ah'm really sorry. Ah've let ye doon."

I said, "Don't worry, Frankie, you've told me now. Let's see how we can get you out of it. I've looked at this situation from every angle and to be honest the only way out of this predicament is if you can manage to get yourself a job, any job, before they phone me back tomorrow morning. If you can manage this then I can say truthfully that there is no such person as you on our books and you're off the hook."

He left the room at a rate of knots.

Next morning he turned up to tell me that he had obtained a job with another building firm. I was obviously delighted but not as much as I was when he followed up by telling me that his cousin, Andy, who was also on our books, equally fraudulently, had managed to find a job with the same firm.

And so, by the greatest of good luck and a little bit of cheeky ingenuity on my part, we managed to keep two trainees out of serious trouble and at the same time get them into work and thus contribute to our success rate.

The only thing I'll never understand about this episode is, how did those two dumbells escape the eagle eye of Lizzie?

Besides Lizzie on the original team we had another woman, Lindsey O'Brien, and two men, Andy McDonald and George Montgomery. Lindsey was omni-competent but functioned mainly as welfare officer for our majority population of single mothers. As such, she was chiefly involved with all aspects of our very important childcare provision and its day-to-day operation. She was also very good at finding placements for our trainees, again particularly our female trainees. Her guidance role was critical to the smooth running of our scheme. She was also the main driver of our college van and I was personally very grateful for this.

Dr Andy McDonald had a PhD in some field of science that I never got fully to the bottom of. He was young and fresh-faced and brought a lot of youthful vitality to the unit. He liked to describe himself as a social terrorist. I never quite knew what he meant by that expression for he was in no way frightening or intimidating and was perfectly well mannered and polite. And, yet, if I think about it, somehow it makes sense. It conveys the idea that he was tremendously audacious in his politics and didn't mind who knew it. He wasn't really that daring in his opinions or his politics but he wanted to be thought so. He proved himself very adept in finding placements, our constant preoccupation, and formed good bonds with our trainees.

George Montgomery was a man in his early sixties who had behind him a very successful career with the National Union of Mineworkers where he had been the top man in the field of health and safety. George had been targeted by the police during the Miners' Strike of the Thatcher years due to his high profile in the NUM and endured many episodes of harassment and aggravation at their hands. He was an extremely likeable individual who inspired trust. He was good to have around the place, because of his great sense of humour but also because of the many stories he could tell of the heroic struggles of the miners and his first-hand accounts of famous figures in the politics of that time.

I remember one memorable story he told about being part of a delegation of senior Scottish trade unionists that were invited to speak at a massive meeting of trade unionists in Russia.

One of the delegates was his friend, Hugh Daly, who was a well-known militant and mightily hated by the right-wing press in Britain. Hugh, like all the other members of the delegation, was a communist. He was a sort of eurocommunist. As such he passionately hated the Stalinist form of communism which he regarded as a debasement, if not the actual antithesis, of pure communism. This was well before glasnost and the fall of the Berlin Wall. At the time of their visit the predominant form of communism in Russia was of the Stalinist sort.

On the flight over Hugh announced to his astonished colleagues that he was going to use the opportunity given him to expose the evils of Stalinism. His colleagues severely cautioned him against such a stupid idea that would be insulting to their Russian hosts, as well as self-defeating and possibly dangerous. Nevertheless Hugh was determined to persist because he genuinely thought that the Russian trade unionists would welcome his remarks, which, he thought, would function as a sort of call to arms of the comrades.

And, indeed, he appeared to be right in this because his address was cheered to the echo and each fresh attack on Stalinism brought forth more and more rapturous applause.

He returned to his seat beside his colleagues with a large smirk on his face. "What did I tell you?" he said.

His colleagues were in a state of total consternation. What they had just witnessed defied belief, and yet it had actually happened. They simply could not make any sense of it.

Then the wily Mick McGahey, the deputy of Arthur Scargill in the NUM, had a brainwave.

He went up to the Kremlin official who had translated Hugh Daly's words to the Russian audience and asked him, "Did you actually tell them what Comrade Daly was saying about Stalinist communism?"

The interpreter replied, "Not at all. Do you think I'm mad? No, I told them that Comrade Daly came from Scotland (applause), the land of Rabbie Burns (thunderous applause) and the home of Rob Roy and William Wallace. I told them of the mountains and glens and of the bonnie, bonnie banks of Loch Lomond. I told them anything and everything I could think of about Scotland and you saw the results, they loved it."

He shifted uneasily for a moment then said, "Is it absolutely necessary for you to tell Comrade Daly about this? I would hate to spoil what was for him such a triumph."

Mick promised to keep it to himself but even as he said it he knew perfectly well that there was no way in the world he could do so.

George Montgomery and Andy McDonald would leave us after a few years. In George's case, this was to spend more time with his wife in retirement and to add to his body of poetry, for George was a published rustic poet of some merit whose poems of mining life showed the influence, and occasionally the magic, of his great idol and inspiration, the immortal Robert Burns. In Andy's case, it was to take up a job introducing the older generation of the area to computers. He called it The Silver Surfers Club.

Their places were taken by two men who would achieve eminence in their own right later. At what we came to call the miners' table arrived David Hamilton who had been imprisoned for his union activities during the Miners' Strike. He was, like George Montgomery, his predecessor, an expert on health and safety.

When we were arranging a placement David would visit the firm concerned to check that all their insurance and health and safety documents were in place. This did not always prove popular with potential placement employers, some of whom resented having to justify themselves to a local community organisation, especially a Craigmillar one. However, it was a risk worth running because you would not believe the great number of companies, including large nationally-known ones, that did not have this documentation in proper order. Some even thanked us for bringing this to their attention, others not so much.

I have no doubt that our punctiliousness in this matter cost us placements but it worked for us very well in terms of reputation and of the satisfaction it gave us in providing a safe environment for our trainees.

The need for this was highlighted amusingly by one inspection we made. It was for a potential clerical placement in a university department. As George Montgomery was entering the premises he could not help casually pointing out that the welcome mat set in the composition floor had worn down and presented a potential safety hazard. They ignored his warning but soon came to regret it, for three weeks later an electrician who was repairing a light at the very same entrance fell off a ladder and broke his leg. The accident, for which they were later held responsible, was a direct result of the fact that the mat did not fit snugly in its container.

This conscientiousness did not just apply to health and safety matters. We kept a close eye on our trainees and their welfare throughout the course of their placement. On one occasion we removed a female trainee from her placement after only two hours on the premises. At her first tea break her employer, in a highly reputable, privately-owned business on the iconic Royal Mile, behaved inappropriately to her. She immediately phoned us and I drove up at once to remove her from the premises and her placement.

Once a senior council official, noticing that a number of our placements were changed during the placement period, opined that we must not be very good at placing them in the first place. I pointed out that this was not only ungenerous but totally false. It was our vigilance in monitoring the placements, and changing them, where necessary, that guaranteed the safety and well-being of our trainees and produced our very excellent exit figures.

Subsequently, David moved on from the People's College to become Member of Parliament for Midlothian, a seat formerly held by the famous Victorian Prime Minister, William Ewart Gladstone. David was later knighted for his services to the Labour Party and trade unionism. Although we can claim no part in his political elevation, we feel justified in thinking that his experience of working in the People's College will have helped him to better understand the problems of the downtrodden in society and, in particular, the contribution that they can make to the body politic.

The other key addition to our staff was Billy McIlheney. Billy, when we first came across him, was an out-of-work actor with a degree in acting who came from the local area. He was very witty and had a great personality. As such he was a great asset, both in the classroom and in the other aspects of our work. Because of his contacts in showbusiness he greatly added to the constant stream of actors and television personalities who not only entertained the trainees but also helped them immensely by taking part in the mock interviews that formed a very important part of our preparation-for-work programme which I have already dealt with.

During his few years with us we, cheekily, gave Billy generous time off to fulfil some short-term filming or recording engagements to allow him to keep his acting career still active. Billy left us, eventually, to take up a principal role in the Scottish soap, *River City*, which is still vastly popular all over Scotland. You could say that Billy, in his way, was also a major success of the People's College, for his 'placement' with us worked a treat in terms of the development of his theatrical career.

TWENTY

Before continuing with our story this might be an appropriate moment to take a peek inside the classroom. The physical layout of the Unit that comprised the People's College consisted of two large rooms that functioned, respectively, as our classroom and our administrative centre or office.

In the commodious office there were five desks; for Lizzie, our secretary, and the four other members of our permanent staff, including myself as manager.

There were two other rooms of more modest dimensions. Just off the office there was a small room that functioned as interview room, confessional and small group venue as the occasion demanded.

Then between the office and the classroom we had our kitchen. The kitchen was undoubtedly the social hub of the whole enterprise. Everything in a sense revolved round it. It was the interface between staff and trainees; it was the studio, when he was with us, of Frank Folan, our unofficial

Artist-in-Residence; from time to time it functioned as a battleground where tiffs and misunderstandings would spill over, play themselves out and be resolved. The kitchen was the beating heart of the whole enterprise and contributed hugely to its smooth working.

The majority of our intake, as I have said before, were women, mostly single mothers. This imbalance in the distribution of the sexes never caused us any problems. Indeed, it worked greatly to our advantage. This was because women, as a group, are generally more practical, down to earth and serious than men and, when left to themselves, can usually be depended upon to get things done.

They were always a force to be reckoned with and even the tough guys in the class were a bit intimidated by them. They could be highly spirited at times. On these occasions their unbridled plain speaking would reach levels of vituperation and ribaldry that no man could cope with.

In their ferocity at times they reminded me of those occasions as a lad growing up in the Vennel when you would come across a group of women dragging a bride-to-be through the streets on her hen night. They were a fearsome sight, dressed as they were, in all kinds of outlandish, pantomime gear and with their faces horribly streaked with garish make-up that gave them a nightmare quality. They resembled nothing more than a group of maenads from Greek mythology as they wandered the streets in search of prey in the form of some unwitting and innocent youth. When one such fell into their clutches, it was said they sometimes did unspeakable things to them, including something fiendish involving a milk bottle that still gives me shivers. The result was that whenever these ghoulish girls-on-the-rampage appeared in the distance, even grown men took to their heels in apprehension, if not outright terror.

I would not say that the women in our successive intakes were actually frightening in that sense but they certainly felt no inferiority to their male counterparts and were a force to be reckoned with when they closed ranks and presented a united front.

There was another way that they could, and did, dominate the male contingent of our group. Raw sexual power.

An example of this was the Great Wonderbra Incident.

It started one day when the normally shy and reticent Margaret Ramage, one of our trainees at the time, took off her coat at the beginning of the lesson to reveal, not her usual modest bosom, but a pair of breasts that would have knocked your eye out. At once, the sisterhood of the women in the class clustered round her, twitteringly, to admire and inspect her 'show' and to ask all sorts of questions about it.

It was in this manner that the class was introduced to the miracle of the Wonderbra that had just come onto the market and would sweep the country for a while. Within a week all the women in the class, it seemed, had succumbed to the temptation that was the Wonderbra. Suddenly our cohort of mainly mammary underachievers was replaced by an army of magnificently-breasted Amazons.

The men in the class were similarly impressed by the spectacular display and clearly enjoyed it, but they did not attempt to exploit its potential for humour, especially of a coarse or vulgar type. Instead they gazed impotently at those mountains, as peasants in a field gaze at a passing lord, amazed and mute.

I would not like you to think that the male members of our community in the People's College were a bunch of shrinking violets. Nothing could be further from the truth. Most of them were people well capable of handling themselves in a fight; some of them had been, till only recently, hardened criminals with police records to match; one of our trainees was an actual murderer – at least one that I know about.

This was a trainee (let's call him Joey) who years after he left us killed a man in a somewhat frenzied manner in a drunken brawl at a New Year's Night party. In the course of the subsequent trial it was conclusively proved that it had been the victim that had brought the knife to the party with the clear intention of doing Joey harm. In the ensuing struggle Joey had wrested the knife from his grasp and then inflicted the wounds that led to his death. The jury, evidently coming to the view that Joey had only acted in self-defence, found him 'not guilty' of the murder.

Though absolved by the court, Joey found it increasingly difficult to absolve himself. He suffered agonies of guilt and remorse at the savage way he had behaved and its consequences and could not forgive himself. He withdrew into his shell and became a bit of a recluse.

Eventually, he took up his religion in a big way and in partial expiation volunteered his services as a part-time gardener in his local parish. He proved to be very skilled in this activity and became jealously protective of the flowers and plants in his care.

One day when he turned up for work the parish priest took him aside to have a word with him and said, "Joseph, we have a problem." Apparently a deer had somehow found its way into the church grounds and was causing some devastation to the flowers and shrubs.

Joey immediately replied, "No, Monsignor, we don't have a problem. But the deer sure has!"

And this proved to be the case for, subsequently, Joey 'dropped the word' in his local hostelry about the incident. Suddenly the deer disappeared from the scene – and was never heard of again.

Still, nothing could assuage, far less overcome, his deep feelings of remorse and guilt. Then one night Joey left his drinking companions at the bar, saying that he was going to have an early night. There was nothing particularly strange or unusual about his leave-taking that night (though some of his friends remembered later the odd detail that he had insisted on shaking everyone's hand as he said farewell on that occasion). Instead of going home Joey went straight to the very high Dean Bridge, and, in a manner that was clearly premeditated, threw himself off the bridge to his inevitable death on the rocks beneath.

I attended his funeral, of course, and it was in many ways a remarkable experience. For a start the church was packed to the gunnels with friends and associates from Craigmillar and the area he lived in before his death. Also present were a sizeable number of suspiciously well-dressed and burly individuals who had the look of big-time Glasgow gangsters.

But the most remarkable thing about Joey's Requiem Mass was the sermon that was preached on the occasion by the parish priest. Though he never mentioned Joey by name or the circumstances of his death, he spoke at great length and movingly about the infinite mercy of God. He stressed that there was no space so exiguous that it could preclude the intervention of the divine mercy of God. The clear implication, understood by all in the church, was that no one could be certain that in the instant between jumping over the bridge and hitting the rocks below Joey could not have managed to seek God's forgiveness – and been given it.

For the theme of his sermon Father Dalrymple, a very saintly and holy man who was known for his ascetic way of life and who, amongst other self-imposed privations, slept on hard boards by way of a bed, chose the story of the Good Thief, otherwise known as the Repentant Thief.

The Good Thief was one of the two malefactors (they were almost certainly not just thieves) that were crucified that day along with Jesus. Taking umbrage at his companion's abuse and derision of Jesus ("He saved others, himself he cannot save"), the Good Thief bade him be silent for, as he pointed out, they deserved what was happening to them whereas Jesus was innocent of any offence.

There was hardly a dry eye in the congregation when Fr Dalrymple concluded his sermon with those truly awesome words that Jesus addressed to the Repentant Thief, "Today you shall be with me in Paradise." What a thank-you present that was!

This was by no means the only funeral of a former pupil that I have attended over the years but it was, without any doubt, the most poignant and dramatic.

Thinking of Joey reminds me of an incident that took place one day as I was arriving for work at the college. I happened to bump into one of our trainees as we were both making our way across the car park to the unit. I had a bone to pick with this particular trainee because he had been absent for the two previous days.

This was a matter of grave concern to me as manager. The one thing on which our co-funders, the Edinburgh City Council and the European Social Fund, most concurred was in the matter of attendance. It was almost a fetish with them. This is understandable because it is only right that people who were, after all, in receipt of public funds should justify them by turning up for work on a regular basis. For this reason I had to supply them annually with the daily attendance sheets of every trainee in the class! It was for me a decidedly irksome task but one I could not shirk because our grant from these authorities hung upon these figures and I could literally not afford any interruption to our funding.

You can well understand why I was so outraged at the trainee who had been absent for two days – and it wasn't the first time! I lost my head with him completely and was 'giving him it tight', as they say in the local patois (sternly rebuking him, to you). I kept jabbing my finger at him as I made my point. He, for his part, simply bowed his head, clasped his hands deferentially behind his back and meekly submitted to my harangue, like a modern-day footballer trying to con the referee into letting him stay on the field after some blatant piece of foul play. The confrontation ended with many apologies on his part and my willing acceptance of them, for the trainee in question was at heart a good lad.

When I had climbed the stairs and entered the office, Lizzie, our secretary, who had witnessed the whole incident from the office window, flew at me in a state of great agitation and exploded:

"What in the name of God is going on in your head? You had me worried sick. Have you any idea who you were talking to?"

"Of course," I replied meekly. "Michael McGurk."

"Aye, Michael McGurk. Otherwise known as Mad Mick. Mad Mick is none other than the leader of the YNT. Do you know who they are, by any chance?" went on Lizzie.

"Yes," I confidently replied. "That's the Young Niddrie Terrors."

"That's right, the Young Niddrie Terrors," responded Lizzie sarcastically. "Only the most notorious gang in Edinburgh. And Mad Mick is the most vicious of them all. And yet you, ya numpty, you see fit to give Mick a hard time and embarrass him – in public! Whit did they teach you at that university?"

Lizzie went on and on at me for some time like a concerned wife – or mother, more like.

As for me, I just clasped my hands behind my back, bowed my head and took it, just like Mick did. After all, we were, neither of us, daft.

TWENTY-ONE

Though our quota of hardmen over the years in the People's College was always high, we had our share of men who were more delicate and refined, like the kind-hearted George McGuigan, the religiously inclined Tom Devanney, our resident artist, Frank Folan, and, of course, our occasional migrants who were in general people of superior refinement and intellect.

You would have thought that our mainly middle-class migrants would have been resented for their difference, not only racially. But it was not so. In fact, they were universally liked and admired by the other trainees. In fact, they were almost proud of them, like the Mafia boss when one of his younger sons decides to become a priest.

Over the years, as you would expect from such a randomly selected group, we had our fair share of oddities and eccentrics.

One such was Marion McNulty, a woman in her early fifties. Marion followed a very strict digestive regime, a forerunner of the modern fad for eating mindfully, which demanded that she chew each mouthful of food a rigorous forty times before swallowing it – and that included milk! As a consequence, to see her eat her lunch was not an edifying sight. I swear to God that in the time it took her to eat a simple sandwich you could have played nine holes of golf.

Then there was Gilbert Royle, known as Slippy, who kept a pet snake in his council flat. It must have been a big snake too, because he fed it a diet of live rats. These were supplied to him by an army of young, local scamps who were excellent and enthusiastic rat-catchers and found rich pickings in the precincts of the defunct Craigmillar Brewery. They provided this service to him at a small fee per rat but I suspect that his suppliers would have been content with the brief glimpse he occasionally permitted them of his snake actually in the act of disposing of one of their captives.

A number of our trainees were strikingly flamboyant in one way or another. There was our 'Geisha Girl', Marie Clare Robb, that I will tell you about later in the story.

Then there was Jim Riddell who had a passionate interest in all things cowboy, hence his nickname of 'Cowboy Joe'. He was a founding member of the local line dancing group and habitually wore cowboy boots, jeans and a broad-brimmed Stetson, even in class. We did not have a dress code as such. The only thing that we insisted on was that no football colours should be worn in class.

Wearing football colours can cause trouble in the religiously divided world of Scottish football. The strongly sectarian element in supporting your team is a phenomenon, peculiar to Scotland, that greatly puzzles outsiders and can even be disconcerting at times to those in the know. This is well exemplified in the little anecdote that follows.

I had just moved from the west of Scotland, the epicentre of religious division, to take up a post teaching in St Anthony's Junior Secondary School in Edinburgh. Being a Catholic school, the vast majority of the pupils were either Celtic or Hibs supporters, though there was always a smattering of Hearts supporters. Hearts was a predominantly Protestant team.

One of these minority Hearts supporters in my first-year class was a bright little spark of a boy called Joe Rowley.

I had just attended my first Hibs v Hearts derby the weekend before. In my time I had attended many matches involving Hibs and Hearts against my own team, Glasgow Celtic, and I had, of course, heard them singing their songs but I had never before heard what they were singing because it was drowned out by the much more massive and vociferous home support. When I heard what the Hearts supporters were singing at that match the day before, I could not wait to bring the matter up with Joe Rowley at the first opportunity.

At the start of the lesson I said to Joe, "Joe, you are a Hearts supporter, aren't you?"

By way of a reply Joe leapt to his feet and proceeded to do

a little dance between the desks while chanting, "Jam tarts. Jam tarts." (Jam tarts is the local rhyming slang for Hearts.)

"Never mind that," I said. "When I was at the match at the weekend your squad were singing anti-Catholic, Rangers-type songs, like 'No Surrender' and 'The Billy Boys'. Do you sing these songs?"

Joe looked at me in a kind of astonishment and said, "Ken, Paddy, ken." (Ken, from the Old English word for 'to know', is a word much used in the Edinburgh dialect and in this case means something like 'of course'.)

"But, Joe," I continued, "after that, they began chanting, 'Fuck the Pope!' Do you chant 'Fuck the Pope'?"

His incomprehension at my stupidity knew no bounds and he just threw his arms wide in a gesture of helplessness and said again, "Ken, Paddy, ken."

I said, "But, Joe, you're a Catholic!"

He threw his hands even wider and said, "What's that got tae dae wi' it?"

I was absolutely dumbfounded and couldn't find the right words to convey my perplexity, so I just contented myself with saying, "Sit down, Joe, you're making me feel like a bigot."

We also had in our ranks from time to time the odd idiot savant. One of these was Wullie Renton. Wullie had failed miserably at school and was barely literate but he was nonetheless a genius at draughts. Draughts, sometimes called 'poor man's chess', is a board game that calls for conspicuous strategic skill in the deployment of pieces or counters. Wullie's superb ability in this game is amply demonstrated in the following story.

Wullie in his youth had been visiting his uncle and auntie in a seaside resort in the north of England. In the course of his peregrinations along the seafront he came upon a group of elderly men who were playing draughts on a board set in the concrete of the pavement with giant-sized pieces that they moved with a stick. They were obviously very skilled and experienced players but whenever any of them made a little mistake, the watching Wullie could not help himself from taking a noisy intake of breath in disapproval. This happened so frequently that the old-timers became irritated by his behaviour. The grizzled old fellow that was the apparent leader of the group couldn't take it anymore and said to Wullie, "Look here, laddie, we've had enough of your sarcasm. Why don't you put your money where your mouth is and play a game against me, if you think you're so smart?"

Wullie apologised for his disrespect and declined the offer at first, saying that he had no wish to butt in. He was eventually persuaded to accept the challenge and took his seat opposite the old fellow. His opponent won the toss and made the first move by moving one of his pieces forward one square. Wullie immediately stood up and said, "That's it. You're beat. I'm off!"

The spectators were aghast and outraged and his opponent said, "What are you talking about? The game's only started. I've just made one move."

Wullie replied, "That's true, but from the position you put yourself in you cannot possibly win. You're beat!"

He was reluctantly persuaded to complete the game after much earnest pleading and some mockery and soon made short shrift of his opponent. They all knew in their hearts this would have happened no matter what initial move his opponent had made.

I think that, given the opportunity, Wullie could have become a master of chess. Perhaps (who knows?) a Grandmaster.

Of course, we had our sad cases too. Margaret, a young woman in her late teens, was one of these. Margaret suffered from narcolepsy which is a debilitating medical condition that caused her to fall asleep inexplicably and uncontrollably at the drop of a hat. This had, obviously, implications for her ability to concentrate on her work in class but it didn't seem to bother her classmates. They had got used to it and just waited for Margaret to 'come to' after each episode and carried on as if nothing had happened.

You could not expect an employer to behave so leniently. We had to remove Margaret early from her 'placement' because, as the placement employer put it, her 'sleeping sickness' constituted a health and safety hazard for herself and her co-workers. Thinking about Margaret still sends shivers down my spine because how would the poor girl cope with bringing up a baby, never mind holding down a job?

It sure keeps things in perspective.

Because of the diverse and problematical backgrounds of our targeted population, we had many instances of mental health problems arising from stress, addiction and social inadequacy. Naturally we did not even attempt to address these medical problems directly or openly. We knew our limitations. We were less a clinic than a centre of meditation and reflection. As such, we could not miraculously solve their mental health problems, but we could ensure that they were better able to cope with them – and that is a kind of miracle.

We had no problems with drug use, as such, on the premises, because it was a binding condition, accepted by all, that to participate in the scheme meant that the trainees had to have put their drug use behind them.

However, sometimes we had problems with the prescribed antidote to heroin, known as methadone. Methadone is a drug widely used by the medical profession to act as a bridge, or, better, as an escape tunnel, between addiction to heroin and complete recovery. It works by administering to the patient initially large doses of the drug to mimic the 'high' and blunt the craving and then, remove the craving entirely by skilfully and steadily reducing the dosage, ultimately to vanishing point.

I am sure that over the years we had a good number of trainees under methadone treatment, but, because of strict doctor/patient confidentiality, we only know for sure of one of them. Because he told us! This trainee, let's call him 'John', was quite open about visiting the clinic every morning before class to receive his daily supervised dose of methadone.

He was, when he was with us, clearly at an early stage in his treatment and still exhibited many signs of going through withdrawal. His concentration levels were poor and he would often go into a kind of a dwam or dreamlike trance, when he would pluck nervously and obsessively at his trouser leg. Apart from this, he presented no problems of any kind in the class and was treated by his classmates with great sympathy and understanding. Nevertheless he abandoned the course early and abruptly without saying why. We can only hope that this decision was taken on sound medical advice, but frankly I doubt it.

If, indeed, there were other methadone users that we did not know about and whose behaviour in class did not raise the suspicion, then we consoled ourselves with the thought that by the law of averages if 85% of our whole intake regularly found employment, then this applied also to them.

Only a very small number of our trainees overall exhibited any signs of marked physical disability, but one of these, called Nellie Coyle, demonstrates very effectively how pointless and demeaning it is to define someone by their impairment.

Nellie had been cursed from birth with a terrible physical defect. She had a withered hand that hung limply and uselessly from the end of her perennially extended right arm and the corresponding leg that she dragged behind her in a piteous and unsightly manner. Remarkably, she was never bitter or self-pitying about her infirmity. As if in compensation, she had been blessed with a good mind and an exceedingly kind and gentle nature. She exuded goodness as a rose wafts perfume and all who knew her were greatly taken by her saintliness. She was the darling of the class, our own Little Flower and a perfect type of St Teresa of Lisieux.

With the help of a friend of the college we got her a job in a small local shop where her quick mind and goodness of nature more than compensated for her disability.

We all miss her still.

TWENTY-TWO

Almost all of our trainees came to the unit with some kind of baggage, as I have explained previously, but the problems that were the most urgent and dramatic were those involving the legal system. Some of our trainees were awaiting trial, some were on remand and some (few) were actually on the run and subject to warrants of arrest. The offences ranged greatly in degrees of seriousness, with shoplifting the predominant offence.

Of course, I was no lawyer and in my attempts to help them could offer nothing more than a plea for leniency. Sometimes I worked through their lawyer, sometimes on my own, but on the whole with a surprising measure of success.

This was partly due to the powerful case I was able to present for the alternative benefits that would accrue to the accused and to the state if they were able to remain with us and continue to rehabilitate themselves through reformative study and work and so become useful members of society.

It was also partly due, I must admit, to the fact that there was sometimes institutional pressure to keep the internment option as a last resort, if possible.

I was, as in so much else in this remarkable story, singularly unfitted for this quasi-legal role because I had never in my life even seen the inside of a courtroom; though I came close to it once, getting as far as the witness room. Here is how it happened.

I was returning from a football match in Glasgow between the deadly rivals, Celtic and Rangers. There were five of us in the car. My brother Eddie and I, plus a friend, called Denis McIvor, and two other brothers, Eddie and Jock Coleman.

Eddie Coleman was driving the car which was a modest but split-new saloon. Eddie's wife had won the car three weeks before in a newspaper competition and had, very reluctantly, allowed her husband to borrow it to take us to the match. She had only agreed to this after much earnest pleading on the part of Eddie and then only after she had extracted from him his solemn promise that he would not touch a drop of drink. Eddie was as good as his word and was perfectly sober. This turned out to be a godsend in more ways than one.

In fact the only person in the car who had taken a lot to drink was Eddie's brother, Jock, who was well-puggled and sat in the driver's passenger seat.

We were proceeding up the main thoroughfare of Byres Road in Partick in a state of great euphoria because Celtic, our team, had just won the match with a goal in virtually the last minute of the game – so, fortuitously.

Suddenly, from a side street and ignoring a stop sign, a powerful Volvo estate, containing, as we later learned, a father and his four children hurtled into us. The Volvo and its acceleration made mincemeat of the front of our small car and deflected by the impact, lodged itself, smoking, in the doorway of a greengrocer's shop right on the corner of the street to the terrified screams of the customers trapped inside.

It was a very dramatic scene: the mangled car, the Volvo embedded in the shop and the screams of the frightened customers. It drew an immediate crowd at that time of a busy Saturday teatime in an area of tall tenements.

The fire brigade and the police arrived very promptly and, using heavy gear, managed to pull open the twisted doors of our little Ford and allow us to get out. All of us, that is, except Jock who was lying face-forward on the dashboard unconscious and covered in blood and couldn't be moved on medical advice.

I went over to the other car to ascertain the well-being of its occupants. All were stunned and shocked but in other respects seemed unharmed. Compliments to Volvo.

As I was returning to our car, now surrounded by a very large crowd, I came upon a Catholic priest that someone must have called to the scene. His church was on the opposite side of the street from the greengrocer's. He was wearing a thin purple stole over his soutane, so he had probably been hearing confessions when he got the call.

I said, "Father, do you want to know if there are any Catholics involved? We are all Catholics on our way back from the match."

Immediately, the cry went up, "The priest! The priest! Make way for the priest!"

The crowd parted like the Red Sea and the priest, with me at his back, walked down the pathway created.

When we reached the car, the priest, who was a bluff, well-built man in his seventies, I would guess, leaned inside and placed the end of his stole tenderly over the shoulder of the comatose Jock.

He said, gently, "My son, I am a Catholic priest."

Jock 'came to' at that moment. He raised his head from the dashboard. His face was like a holy picture, streaked with blood and cuts and pitted with broken glass from the windshield.

The priest said to him, "My son, you were very lucky."

"I know, Father, I could have been killed," said the forlorn Jock.

"No. At the match, I mean," said the priest.

I thought, a little roguishly, once a Celtic supporter, always a Celtic supporter, priest or no priest!

Subsequently, the driver of the Volvo was charged with dangerous driving and, against all the evidence, chose to plead 'not guilty'. As a result we were all called to the High Court in Glasgow as witnesses.

By this time Jock's face was back to normal as his wounds had been merely superficial; I think the drink taken might have helped there. They say, don't they, that God looks after the drunk.

After two hours or so of waiting to be called, a court official came and told us that we could go home now as the driver had decided to plead guilty, undoubtedly in response to the impassioned pleas of his quivering lawyer. We were all given compensation for loss of earnings and spent the rest of the day between Glasgow and our hometown of Dumbarton imbibing on the strength of the compensation without fear of reproach or censure from spoilsport spouses.

Over the years I handled cases in an assortment of courts and, since success breeds success, quickly acquired a reputation for this work, even amongst the legal fraternity. I was frequently asked by lawyers, whom I did not know, to help put together a mitigation plea for their own clients. I always refused because, as I told them, I didn't even do it for all my own people but only for those that I was convinced would respond to it and not let me down. It would make no sense to write something like that in the abstract and without detailed knowledge of the personalities involved.

One case gave me particular pleasure for its long-term outcome. The case involved a young woman who had a terrible history of drug addiction and recurrent offending. This had led to her serving two years in the notorious women's prison of Corton Vale. When she came to my attention she was facing 132 outstanding cases of shoplifting. These crimes were committed in all areas of Scotland from Aberdeen to the Borders. She was so notorious in her profession that her photograph was in the Rogues Gallery in the staffrooms of all the big stores in Edinburgh and Glasgow. *If you see this woman in the store, call security immediately*.

The court where she was to appear to answer the charges was in Edinburgh and all the charges were presented as one, in an arrangement even the lawyers call a 'roll-up'. I had only ever known this expression in its gambling connotation where it means an accumulator bet.

By this time she was on our books and had put her drug use behind her and was seriously trying to rebuild her life and that of her two children with our help and support. I was perfectly convinced, against all the odds, that she would respond well to any leniency afforded her.

To cut a long story short, the sheriff was impressed – and possibly a little intrigued – with the prospect of what we could do for her, if she was not to be removed from our midst. I think also that he may have thought, *This woman is a hopeless recidivist. We have tried everything with her and it has failed. What have we got to lose by trying this?*

For whatever reason, he decided to release her into our recognisance with the provision that if at the end of her time with us she had not reoffended and that we could give a similarly favourable report on her progress then the charges against her would be quashed – which, in fact, they were.

The really wonderful thing about this case, in both senses of the word, is that Marilyn, for that was the young woman's name, not only got herself a permanent job with our help but also, as you will discover, in one of the last places you would imagine. So far as I am aware all these years later she went on to make a good life for herself and her children and fully justified our faith and that of the sheriff in her redemption.

This formula of holding back the nullification of the charges until we had made a satisfactory report on the progress and success of the individuals involved became almost routine for us and enhanced our reputation more generally, as well as encouraging our trainees to fearlessly bring their problems to us. The fact that their failure to respond positively to such a great opportunity would impact severely not only on themselves but, just as significantly, on their colleagues and friends who might have reason later to profit from similar opportunities, was a big factor in their determination not to let the side down. It had the concomitant effect of intensifying the esprit de corps of our tight little community which was our greatest strength.

It goes without saying that everything wasn't always plain sailing. We had our setbacks. I remember one such setback very vividly. It was particularly upsetting because it seemed a case we could not lose; a slam-dunk case, if you ever saw one.

We discovered that one of our new trainees, who had come to us from the local women's refuge, had an outstanding fine, unpaid for more than a year, and that there was a warrant out for her arrest.

She wasn't our usual type of person. She did not come originally from Craigmillar. Geographically and culturally she was a complete outsider. Her father was a banker in an affluent area of Edinburgh. Besides, or possibly because of, being a fish out of water she was incredibly shy and insecure.

It turned out that she was on the run from an abusive partner whose physical abuse of her had earned him a three-year jail sentence (no small sentence when you consider the leniency which courts display all too often towards men in domestic abuse cases). When he was released from prison on completion of his sentence, for fear of him, she was forced to go on the run. She had lived in various women's refuges across the Borders before finding herself in the refuge in Craigmillar.

Because of her basic poverty and the enforced frequent changes of address she had failed to keep up her promise to the court to pay in instalments the fine of £100 previously imposed on her. This was the reason for a warrant being issued for her arrest.

When she explained the situation to me I was completely untroubled for, of course, we would undertake to pay the outstanding amount which we would recover later from her 'wages'. So, on my advice, she turned herself in and a court date was appointed. In my innocence I thought that it would be a simple procedure. I would go into the court, explain the circumstances to the sheriff, pay the fine and that would be that.

However, while I was giving this encouraging message to my trainee, a court policeman in the vicinity leaned over to me and said, "I am sorry, sir, but I couldn't help overhearing your conversation. You are making a big mistake going into court. I know this sheriff and he is dead set against anyone but a qualified lawyer appearing before him. He's a real hard bastard. You would be better getting one of the court-appointed duty solicitors to present the case. There are always plenty of them around."

I thanked him for his well-intentioned advice. The young woman and I discussed the matter. She was in such a complete state of funk that she was not prepared to do anything that carried the slightest risk. I was perfectly at ease about this. After all, it was a slam-dunk case and I had no particular ambition to play a lead role in the proceedings.

It did not prove difficult to find a court-appointed lawyer.

When he arrived, he was utterly unprepossessing. Indeed, if anything, he looked untidy and a bit scruffy. Moreover, his personality proved a perfect match for his charmless appearance for he was arrogant and patronising.

He asked my trainee why it was that she had stopped paying her fine.

The young woman was incoherent with fear and embarrassment so I began to explain about the violent husband, her flight from him and the successive women's refuges.

He cut me short and said, "Sorry, Mr McLaughlin, I'm the lawyer here and I know what I am doing. So, please leave it to me."

I backed off at once and if my eyebrow raised up a little I don't think anybody noticed.

Then he asked her how she could manage to pay the fine. The young woman just looked at him blankly.

I came in again and explained that we paid her a weekly wage and so we would be able to pay the fine for her and recover it from her wages. At least that is what I would have said if he hadn't stopped me before I could get going and said, "Mr McLaughlin, I know you mean well but I must insist that you do not interfere when I am speaking to my client."

At this point I had no option but to stay out of things and so I backed off, this time for good.

Eventually, the case was called.

I was in the spectators' gallery, behind a wall of reinforced glass, to watch the proceedings.

After a few routine questions the sheriff asked, "Why has your client failed to comply with the court order to pay this fine?"

Our apology for a lawyer replied, "I don't know, Your Honour."

When he was asked what were her circumstances and how could she manage to pay the fine in future our hero answered once again, "I don't know, Your Honour."

At this the sheriff, who seemed to have some anger-management issues, went into a towering rage.

"I am sick to the back teeth," he said, "of feckless people who refuse to take responsibility for their obligations. I will not tolerate it. You have offered no explanation for your failure to pay this fine and have given no assurance as to your willingness to pay it in future. I have had enough of this kind of mockery of the law. I'm afraid a custodial sentence seems to be the only option."

At this, I launched myself against the reinforced glass at the front of the gallery and yelled, "Bastard!"

Even the hardened 'friends of the accused' who were my fellow spectators were alarmed at my demonstration. A policeman pulled me back from the glass and warned me that if I did not sit down quietly I would find myself under arrest for a very serious breach of the peace. I realised at once that this would have a devastating effect on my future relations with the court and on any of my trainees who might have occasion to depend on them.

I sat down.

Meanwhile, the sheriff, before passing sentence, had discovered that my trainee was a single mother with a child that day in nursery and so it would be impossible to pass a custodial sentence in the circumstances. Very reluctantly, he adjourned the case to a later date.

From watching cases like this, I knew that it was customary for the defence lawyer to leave the court with his client. This time the lawyer, her lawyer, slipped out by a back door so flush with the wall as to be almost invisible and left his client abandoned in the well of the court.

I hurried down to join her. We then went to the cashier's desk in the building. In a matter of minutes I had paid the total of her liabilities by a personal cheque which I would recover from college funds later and sent her on her way home a very relieved woman.

After she had gone I found that my anger at the crass stupidity and arrogance of her lawyer had not abated since my attempted assault on the glass partition. I proceeded to go round and round the passageways of the court, like a lion in search of prey, trying to find the lawyer who had come so close to putting an innocent young woman in prison through his idiocy and indifference. Without the slightest doubt, I would have put him up against a wall, if I had found him.

My anger must have been evident to the court functionaries I kept passing. Eventually, one female police officer asked me what I was doing. I told her briefly what had happened and said I wanted a serious word with the lawyer in question. She became very alarmed and pointed out to me that this could have serious repercussions for me. She was not at all unsympathetic to me but, nevertheless, insisted on accompanying me to the front of the building and sending me on my way.

But the case that was the most daunting – and proved the most famous in our history – happened not long after this near disaster and merits fuller treatment in a chapter of its own.

TWENTY-THREE

It all started one Thursday morning when one of my trainees in placement with a firm of builders turned up, unexpectedly, at the college and asked to speak with me in private. He was visibly upset and trembling as he spoke.

"Paddy," he said, "I'm in real stook and I don't know where to turn. Can you help me, please?"

He then went on to tell me that he had been sentenced some time ago to a period of three months in prison (I didn't know that). He had immediately put in an appeal against the sentence and this appeal was coming up the very next day at the Court of Appeal.

Because you can only appeal a conviction if some error had been made in the original trial or if fresh evidence arises that could have affected the original sentence (and neither of these applied in this circumstance), his case was hopeless. As a result his lawyer refused to go with him to the court. This was entirely understandable for the simple fact of officiating in the highest court in the land would have been daunting for any lawyer without the highest skills and the requisite experience. But for a novice without a leg to stand on?

Moreover, my trainee, who went by the street-name of Amigo, had been refused legal aid and so would be forced to confront his ordeal totally without support.

I told him plainly that there was nothing I could do for him as his case was unwinnable. I further told him that this court would not even listen to me.

However, seeing how upset and trembling he was – he really didn't fancy three months in jail at all – I could not leave him in the lurch. I told him that, at the very least, I would write a letter on his behalf to the court. I warned him that almost certainly they would not even read it but it would be, at least, something. He was happy with this and particularly with my promise to attend the court with him.

I set about writing a mitigation plea for him. I explained who I was. I made it explicitly clear at the outset that I had no doubt he was guilty as charged and that the sheriff was doing no more than his proper duty in giving him the sentence that he did. I went on to say a few words about the People's College and the redemptive aspects of our work. I related in detail how, though virtually illiterate when he first came to the People's College, he was learning to read and write. He had recently got back in touch with his long-estranged father by letter and, through a difficult and awkward correspondence, he and his father were growing closer. I said that it was my firm belief that I could do more for this young man and his rehabilitation as a useful member of society than any prison term could and begged them to give him and us the chance to bring this about.

Even as I wrote it, I knew it would cut no ice with the court.

The next morning Amigo said farewell to his weeping, elderly mother at the door of the house he would not see again for three months. Then he set off with in his possession only a small tin containing enough tobacco to serve his immediate needs in prison and a few coins. He had been well advised by knowledgeable friends who told him that any more than this minimum could attract unwelcome attention from the wrong kind in prison.

At about the same time, and before my appointed meeting with Amigo and the official beginning of the day's session, I handed in my typewritten statement to the court. From long-standing perspicacity I kept it to an easy-to-read, single-sided sheet.

After I handed in the submission I remained in court to watch the proceedings for a while. Amigo's case would not be called for some hours yet and I wanted to be able to advise him as best I could.

The first thing that surprised me was how short a time it took to dispense with the majority of cases. I quote one as an example.

The appellant emerged from the particular court entrance that bespoke the fact that he was already serving a sentence in prison. He was an unprepossessing figure of a man and slouched lazily against the rail of the dock as if he were at home in his own kitchen. Furthermore, like most guilty people, he mumbled when he spoke.

When asked his name by the senior judge, he muttered something inaudible.

Irritated, the judge said to the bailiff, "What did he say?"

The bailiff replied in a loud voice, "He said his name is John Caldwell, Your Lordship."

"And on what grounds are you appealing?" barked the judge.

Yet again, the appellant mumbled something incoherent.

The judge, angry now, again addressed his bailiff, "What did he say?"

The bailiff translated for him and said, "He claims that the sheriff who passed sentence on him knew him.

The judge angrily riffled through a file of sheets thick as a fat book and curtly said, "There isn't a sheriff in Scotland that doesn't know you. Case dismissed."

It had taken all of two or three minutes from first to last! My heart sank lower and lower.

Nevertheless, it had given me some things to mull over with Amigo when we caught up.

By custom, the advocates and their clients walk up and down Advocates' Hall in opposite parallel lines to the other advocates/clients to allow them to discuss things in confidence. I, of course, did not have this privilege, nor the cheek to arrogate it; so Amigo and I walked round and round outside in the open air in the nearby Parliament Square.

I told him that when he went into the box he must stand bolt upright as if he was in the Cadet Corps or the Boys' Brigade. As if! In addition, he must shout out his answers in a loud voice, really shout.

"You'll think you're shouting," I said, "but they'll hear you just lovely."

I hinted that, being old men, the hearing of the judges might not be what it once was.

I reiterated to him that it was most likely that they would not even read my letter, but, on the off-chance that they did, we must prepare ourselves for any questions that could emerge. They were, for the most part, predictable: 'What is the People's College?'; 'What sort of stuff are you doing there?'; 'What could it lead to?'.

We prepared answers to these questions that we felt sure would not be asked and then, as we always did, we rehearsed these answers. At least it kept us from worrying and allowed the time to pass relatively quickly.

When Amigo's case was called, I saw the bailiff hand over my letter to the senior judge. There were three of them all dressed in scarlet and ermine. After the senior judge had read the submission, he invited the other two judges to lean closer and read it together in their turn. My heart began to beat a little less clamorously. So far, so good.

Then the senior judge asked if Mr McLaughlin was in court. I stood up expectantly. However, he seemed satisfied by my mere presence and went on to question Amigo who was by this time standing virtually to attention.

Just as I had predicted, the senior judge asked all the questions to which we had already prepared answers. Amigo, when he got into his stride, was magnificent. His account of the reconciliation with his father would have brought a tear to a glass eye. I had hinted to him that, you never know, perhaps even judges have sons or daughters that don't keep as much in touch as they should. A hint like that was all that Amigo needed. It was his finest hour, and, oh, how he relished it!

The judge, after a brief conversation with his colleagues, proceeded to berate Amigo for his persistent and heinous offences and said that the prison sentence he had been given was the least he could have expected.

My heart began to beat just a little faster.

Amigo remained motionless as a statue.

Then the judge said, "Despite what I have already said about your guilt, we are going to do something unusual. Something I am not even sure we have the right to do. But we're going to do it anyway. We are going to put you back into Mr McLaughlin's custody (I thought 'care' might have been a more felicitous term but, perhaps, he wanted it to seem as severe as possible). If you put your life in order and do not reoffend and provided that Mr McLaughlin can write an equally positive report on your progress at the end of your time with the People's College, your conviction will be quashed at that time."

Amigo and I were too stunned to react and it was only when we had retired to a nearby bar and I got him a few stiff whiskies that we both found it possible to comprehend the astonishing thing that had just happened back there in that court.

Then Amigo left by bus to return, three months earlier than expected, to his home in Craigmillar. For obvious reasons he had not seen fit to take his keys with him when he left that morning, so he had to ring the bell.

When his old mother eventually opened the door and saw her son smiling stupidly in front of her, she exclaimed: "My God, Amigo, what have you done? Have you escaped?"

Naturally this story became an overnight sensation in the legal community and boosted my already high reputation as the mitigator supreme.

TWENTY-FOUR

I mentioned earlier in the work that, as a resident of the Vennel in Dumbarton in the west of Scotland, I came from the same deprived background as many of my former pupils. I acknowledged at that time that the poverty of my childhood was mitigated and explained how.

Nevertheless, it was still pretty dire.

I grew up in a room-and-kitchen, called a single-end. A single-end was the basic and most prevalent architectural unit in the crowded tenements of the urban poor. It consisted of two rooms: a main room that functioned as reception area and kitchen as well as the bedroom of my parents (which was nothing more than a bed set into a recess in the wall, enclosed by a curtain for privacy), and a small adjoining room containing some hooks by way of a wardrobe and a bed in which my two brothers and I slept, under an additional blanket of coats in the coldest weather.

In the main room there was an old range which had long since fallen into disrepair due to the neglect of the landlord and functioned now only as an open fire on which we cooked our meals. Inadequate as it was, it was the only source of heat in the apartment. The only other furniture in the main room consisted of a table and some chairs and a single armchair which was at the sole disposal of my mother when my father was at work and we boys were at school. It became my father's exclusive province when he returned home exhausted after a hard day's shift at the shipyard. Because he was engaged in essential warwork, my father was exempt from military service, though he had served for a short time in the navy, as a lad, at the tail end of the First World War.

There was no electricity or running hot water in the apartment. Light was provided by means of a gas mantle and all water had to be heated in a large pot over the open fire. A gas mantle was a very fragile thing and required great finesse in attaching it to the gas pipe. Even then, the light it provided was feeble and flickering, though in truth it never seemed to bother us at the time. As with all the other privations of wartime Britain we got used to it and, knowing no better, we just got on with it and did the best we could.

The greatest privation we endured was the lack of a toilet inside the apartment. The only toilet available to us and the other four families who shared our space on that floor of the tenement was what was called a 'stairheed toilet', a stairheed being in the vernacular the small communal entrance lobby at the top of a flight of stairs. There were, of course, similar lobbies above and below us in that tall tenement.

The stairs were also lit by gas but it was usually dark, especially at night, because the communal gas lamps were poorly maintained (again) by the private landlord who owned the building. I was a highly sensitive and imaginative child and when I was coming home after dark I had great fear of the monsters that I was convinced were lurking in the shadows of the stairs ready to seize me.

I would hesitate outside the mouth of the close, or long entrance to the tenement, to pluck up my courage and then, I would take a very deep breath and, shouting "O-P-E-N!" at the pitch of my voice, I would launch myself in and race up the stairs in the hope that someone in our house would respond to my cry and open the door for me. This would provide me with the light needed to reach the door safely and would effectively dispel the evil creatures that I knew could not stand the light, and thus prevent them from seizing me in their unholy grasp.

I subsequently learned that I was not the only boy of my age to have this phobia. Even the tough guys in the tenement – and there were plenty of them, I can tell you – did not forbear to shout "O-P-E-N!" when the occasion demanded it. This strategy had the merit that you could pass it off as due to no more than a great urgency to be home rather than fear of the dark.

However, I knew it for what it was and so did every other boy in the stair.

The communal toilet was very primitive, to say the least, and was generally very insalubrious, mainly due to old Mrs Muldoon who had dementia and could not look after herself properly. As a result, I seldom, if ever, used it, being forced to use a po or chamber pot instead.

I don't even like thinking about this, as it brings back very uncomfortable memories. In this sense, I was not at all like the small boy in the story that follows that says as much as I feel like saying on a subject so unedifying and distasteful.

One day an officer of the gas board seeking entrance, perhaps to read a meter or the like, knocked on the door of one of these stairheed closets, mistaking it for the door of one of the dwellings. After he had knocked several times, more and more persistently, a small boy's voice came from behind the door saying:

"I'm in here. What do you want?"

The gas man said, "Is your father in? I would like to talk to him."

The boy answered, "He left when ma maw came in."

The gas man continued, "Well, can I speak to your mother, please?"

"No. She left when ma Uncle Joe came in."

"Well him, then," persisted the exasperated gas man.

"You can't. He left when ah came in."

At this the gas man lost all patience and exploded, "In the name of God, what kind of house is this at all?"

The small boy replied, "It's a shithouse, ya bam."

There was a remarkable camaraderie among the residents of the tenement. You never had to lock your door. If a neighbour chose to visit the house, the first you knew about it was when you heard them knock on the door and simultaneously open it saying, "Are ye in, Mary?"

There was, of course, the odd stairhead row, now and then, and these could be incandescent while they lasted. However, they generally blew themselves out pretty quickly and an even closer harmony would follow.

Worse were those concealed animosities that never flared into outright conflagration but smouldered slowly and malignantly in the background. Our next-door neighbour was the not-innocent victim of this.

She was a fine-looking but difficult woman who was greatly disliked by all the other neighbours. Except, that is, for my mother who got on very well with her in the main.

She was mostly despised for the airs she gave herself. She came originally from Edinburgh and thought herself superior to everyone else on the stair for this reason and because she had a brother who was a priest. The first reason cut no ice with anyone but herself and merely justified the neighbours in their animosity towards her. The fact that she had a brother 'in the cloth', as they used to say, did, however, carry great cachet value in our strongly Irish Catholic community.

I was the same age as her only child, Aidan, and we got along quite well, although we were never really close friends. As a result of my usefulness to her as a companion for her only son, Mrs McConnachie showed some preference for me over my younger brothers, but, in truth, I did not really like her all that much. It seemed to me that she took advantage of my mother.

It was not uncommon for her to turn up at our house around teatime, particularly at weekends. My mother always made something pretty special on a Saturday night, usually involving steak, for my father. It functioned as an appreciation for all his hard work during the week and the wage he provided so constantly. However, I am sure that it was also intended to constitute an inducement to stay in and not go out to the pub. If this was so, it never worked. Deep down nobody minded this really because my father was a good drunk and the family atmosphere was always cheery when he returned from the pub in a good mood with, usually, two or three companions as amiable as himself. Oh, what nights we had then!

But to get back to Mrs McConnachie. She would inevitably turn up when something nice was sizzling in the pan. She would say, "That looks nice, Mary," then pick up a piece of the steak or whatever it was and say, "I'll just take a wee bit for Jimmy's (her husband) tea."

I used to hate it when she did that but my mother was too nice to take offence, though I knew deep down she didn't like it.

But I hated it even more when it happened to me!

One day in school I quoted some things from a book I had found on our mantlepiece at home. It was a religious book for the instruction of young seminarians. This book had been given to my mother some time before by Mrs McConnachie, no doubt to impress upon my mother the difference between their two respective environments, hers in polite and cultured Edinburgh and ours in darkest Dumbarton. She used her brother's position in the church to patronise my mother.

Of course, it didn't work on her any more than it worked on me. My mother sailed too high in the sky to be reached by the feeble arrows of snobbery or pretension. She accepted the book from her friend at face value and took from it what she could, for she had an absolute lust for self-improvement. Basically, she was just a nice person.

I also found the book fascinating and read it avidly for I was always deeply religious, like my mother. I don't know which part of it I was recounting in class that day, but it certainly caught the attention of our teacher, Mr O'Hanlon. He expressed an interest in seeing it for himself and I said I would get it for him when I went home at lunchtime and bring it in in the afternoon.

Now it so happened that Aidan McConnachie was in the same class as me and witnessed the conversation between me and the teacher. He suspected that the book came from his mother's collection. He at once set off, at a run, to relate everything to his mother. She immediately went into my mother and requested the return of the book in question.

When I turned up, eventually, at the house, for I was always last in everything, a real slouch, I at once began searching frantically for the book. Of course, I didn't find it for it was gone already. I was really, really upset. It was my big chance to impress Mr O'Hanlon and I didn't want to lose it.

Eventually, my mother, noticing my frantic activity, asked me, "What's wrong, Pat? What are you looking for?"

I said, "That book I was reading. You know, the one you got from Mrs McConnachie. Do you know where it is? I need to bring it to school to let the teacher see it."

My mother looked pained for a moment and I saw a darkness grow at the back of her eyes that I knew from experience did not portend well for who had prompted it.

She simply said, "Mrs McConnachie came in just now to take the book back. It was her book so I had no right to refuse."

It was all I could do to stop myself from crying with self-pity and anger. I cursed in my heart the cold-hearted, stuck-up bitch that was Mrs McConnachie and her wily little sneak of a son, Aidan.

The afternoon was a disaster. Aidan produced the book proudly as his own and claimed all the credit for it that should have been mine. Though he said nothing at the time I knew that Mr O'Hanlon was not fooled by what happened that day.

He said to me much later, "Remember this, Pat, a book belongs not to who merely owns it, not even to who wrote it, for it has passed on publication from his hand and belongs to the world of books. There, the author is no more than a reader of his own work like any other reader. It belongs solely and forever to the reader who is sensitive to its magic. That book was yours that day as surely as my name is Matt O'Hanlon and don't let anyone tell you any different. Now go and plunder the literature of the world: it's yours for the taking!"

The respect for the cloth that I referred to earlier was exemplified perfectly on those occasions, every two months or so, when Mrs McConnachie's brother, Father Peter, as we called him, would come to visit her from his parish in Edinburgh.

In those days, although everyone in the tenement, including the McConnachies, was poor, even the poorest had at least one household item that was pretty decent and was treasured almost as a family heirloom. It might have been a bit of carpet, a cutlery set, an embroidered tablecloth or a pair of candlesticks from a sickbed set. They guarded them jealously and took them out only on the most special occasions.

On the night before a projected visit of Father Peter – and how did they know? – the neighbours would silently lay their most treasured possessions in a heap at Mrs McConnachie's door. She, for her part, would take them in and use them to decorate her house and make it fit for the visit of a priest. After he had gone, she would leave the items in a pile outside her door to be retrieved by their owners. So far as I know, not a word passed between the benefactors or the beneficiary on these occasions. There was nothing personal in it, gratitude did not apply. It was done solely out of a deep respect for the priesthood and the recognition that he was visiting, per force, not only his sister but also the little community of neighbours that she lived among.

There was one neighbour between whom and Mrs McConnachie there subsisted a vicious and reciprocal animosity, amounting almost to a hatred. This woman, Maggie Rainey was her name, used to shout at and abuse Mrs McConnachie whenever they saw each other. She would say things like 'You're daft, McConnachie, daft. Dae ye hear me?'

Poor Maggie was not quite right in the head and was truly the poorest of the poor. She had nothing whatsoever of value to put on the pile to honour Father Peter's visit. However, she did have something very special that she could contribute and she happily did so.

Maggie, on the morning of the visit, would get up early and wash both flights of stairs leading up to Mrs McConnachie's door and, for good measure, the flight leading up from it. Not only that! Maggie was an absolute wizard with a bar of pipeclay and would chalk oriental designs of leaves and flowers on each end of the newly-washed steps, so that it looked for all the world like a monochrome Persian runner carpet. It was an absolute work of art. And to do all that, at least parenthetically, for someone you hate with all your heart says everything about the quality and worth of Maggie. It says it also about the whole community, not only of our tenement but of all the other tenements like it in the Vennel.

TWENTY-FIVE

The teacher I had in the two years preceding my qualifying class with Mr O'Hanlon was a massive influence on my future life. Andy Powell was a giant of a man from the Ring of Kerry in the west of Ireland.

He was big in every way: big in his eloquence and imagination and big, as well, in his flaws and prejudices. He was an ardent Irish Nationalist and had a fierce hatred for the English. This hatred did not exclude the English nun who was our headteacher. This woman was unquestionably a strict disciplinarian. Nothing escaped her eagle eye. Or her censure. In her zeal for her work she used to visit – or at least pass through – every classroom in the school every day, morning and afternoon, religiously, you might say.

Whenever she came into our room, if he himself was speaking, he would stop at once, fold his arms aggressively on his chest and look at her silently with a curled lip till she had passed through the other door en route to her office. If one of us kids happened to be speaking at the time, he would silence us at once with an upraised hand the size of a ham. Every day, twice a day, for the two years I was in his class, he would say the same thing when she left the room:

"Did you see that, boys?" he would say. "Did you see that bitch swishing her English skirts at me?"

In truth I did not see that. All I saw was a somewhat apprehensive woman, her feet like two wee black mice, scurrying across the room to escape his fearsome contempt.

In Andy's class all the history we got was Irish history and not the Ireland of Saints and Scholars but the Ireland of heroes and rebels and the martyred dead. At the drop of a hat he would march up and down the front of the class, using his pointer as a makeshift rifle, and sing at the top of his considerable voice 'Kelly the boy from Killane' or 'The Bold Fenian Men'.

In his lessons he mixed historical fact and myth with great aplomb. His stories were peopled by real heroes of the Irish struggle, like Robert Emmet, Wolfe Tone and Patrick Sarsfield but intertwined with them would be mythical figures like Cuchulain, Fionn mac Cumhaill and Oisin. All comported happily in a great seething, almost mystical, mass.

I remember with remarkable clarity his account of the Battle of Clontarf; in his opinion the greatest battle in the history of the world, bar none. This was the battle in which the hitherto invincible Vikings, who had wreaked havoc for hundreds of years along all the littorals of Europe and North Africa, suffered their first defeat – at the hands of the Irish under their High King, the eighty-year-old Brian Boru.

Here are the very words I heard as an enthralled ten-year-old all those years ago and that have rung in my imagination ever since:

"Der de were, boys, on the mornin' of that great battle. Dese dirty great Danes wid their spears stickin' in the air like fields of wavin' corn as far as the eye could see. And dere was Brian Boru and two or three o' the fellas…"

It was epic. It was magnificent. It sure fired my blood and my imagination. Of course, it prepared me for no examination I could ever conceive of, but it did open to me later, I am sure, the door to the world of Homer, Milton and Shakespeare. Thanks, Andy, for that and for so much more.

The bond between us even survived the crushing blow to our relationship that I am about to recount and in which there was a good deal of fault on both sides.

Briefly, in the middle of a lesson, Andy realised that I had disengaged myself from the lesson and was surreptitiously reading a book of some kind under my desk. At this perceived insult to his teaching Andy flew into a very Irish rage and proceeded to deliver to me the mother and father of all dressing-downs right in the face of the whole class. It was humiliating in the extreme. But worse was to follow.

To my great surprise and horror he later reported the incident to Sister Hilda, our much-feared headteacher. I didn't even know that they spoke to each other, but I suppose they had to on occasion, didn't they?

Sister Hilda immediately communicated what had happened to my mother. Now, whether through malice on someone's part or simple bad luck in the transmission, by the time the story got to my mother it was my mother's understanding that I had been reading 'a dirty book' in class.

This was so gross a piece of misconduct on my part as to merit the severest chastisement. She immediately reached out for her carpet beater and proceeded to give me several sharp whacks across the back of my bare legs. My mother was the most amiable of people and a very loving mother but where morality or, especially, immorality was concerned she could be fearsomely strict.

I was a bit of a goody two shoes and so did not have much experience of this extreme form of chastisement. By contrast, my two younger brothers were always getting up to mischief and so had more experience than I of the carpet beater. This was particularly true of my nearest brother in age, Eddie, who had such an intimacy with the instrument of castigation that years later, and after the death of our mother, he hung the carpet beater in question among his holy pictures on the wall, like a relic, in loving memory of our mother. I suppose that if some Italian had discovered, or thought he had, the actual scourge that had been used on Jesus that day in Pilate's courtyard he would have done no less.

As for all that stuff about 'a dirty book', it was a piece of nonsense. The book was called *Escape from Dartmoor* and was a Boy's Own type of derring-do fiction that told the story of a daring and successful escape from the notorious and popularly-supposed escape-proof prison on Dartmoor. There was nothing in the smallest degree salacious or immoral in the content or the language of the story, so where the idea of 'dirty' came from is anybody's guess.

Of one thing I am perfectly sure. If the story had been about the escape of some Fenian prisoner from an English jail, I would have heard no more about it. Unless it was to commend me for my astute and enterprising time-management skills.

It is easy to see from all the foregoing that the community of the Vennel was not deprived culturally or educationally. In fact, the Vennel was sometimes known as 'university alley' for the surprising number of university graduates it produced; most of them teachers, several priests of course, and two actual bishops.

Just at this minute it has occurred to me that there is something deliciously apposite about this strong clerical tradition. The Vennel (pronounced locally Vinil) was the name of our street for successive generations but its official or real name was College Street because it was built on the site of the medieval, pre-Reformation and, therefore Catholic, Collegiate Church of St Mary, the ancient patroness of the town.

The Vennel also boasted a published author in the person of John Joseph Boylan who had written some successful cowboy books, one of which was made into a B-movie western. It defies belief how he managed to conjure up the bluffs and canyons of Colorado from the tall tenements and dark back greens of the Vennel where he had lived all his life. But he did!

Johnjo was a good deal older than me and a grown man but I knew him perfectly well, both as a member of our tight-knit community and as a celebrity in his own right.

He was unusual for another reason, for his nickname (everyone had nicknames at that time) was 'Shirley'. This sobriquet in no way implied any ambiguity about his sexuality. In fact Shirley was a notorious womaniser and his frequent visits to the big city of Glasgow were, it was darkly hinted, for no innocent purpose. No, it turns out that his nickname came from the fact that he was extremely handsome, too good-looking for a boy, it was thought.

I had only ever one conversation with John Joe Boylan in my entire life, but it was a notable one.

I was about twelve at the time and was gazing lustfully and uselessly at the delightfully technicoloured display of confectionery in the window of Rocchiciolli's Sweetie Shop. Pocket money hadn't been invented yet, at least not in the Vennel, so I could get no further than looking through the window at the paradise inside. Suddenly, Shirley Boylan appeared at my side and, perfectly aware of who I was and of the very devout family from which I came, he opened a conversation with me, saying, "I'm an atheist, you know."

I was rendered delirious with shock. An atheist? In the Vennel? It was beyond staggering. I could not comprehend how anyone could be so audacious as to refuse to believe in God. I must say that shocked though I was, I was even more impressed. It was as if he had casually told me that he had just that minute stepped off a spaceship from the planet Mars. He was a marvel in my eyes.

Of course, I was aware, even at the time, that he was, in a kindly way, testing me, trying to get a reaction. I also knew, instinctively, that he was doing so because he liked me and saw something of his former self in me.

I can't remember what happened next. I was too flabbergasted to conjure up a response and he, for his part, having achieved his objective, just walked away, or dematerialised, as it seemed to me.

I don't know what became of him subsequently.

Where do old cowboy writers go to die?

Thinking about my life in the Vennel and the hidden values it managed to nurture and progress, greatly comforted me and sustained me in my later work in Craigmillar; for the comparisons between Craigmillar and the Vennel were only too easy to identify.

The estate of Craigmillar had been selected as an area for the rehousing of the urban poor in the sixties. The locality from which most of the new residents of Craigmillar had been transferred, holus-bolus, was the area of dark tenements clustered around the church of St Patrick's in the densely crowded Cowgate district of Edinburgh. As such, they were, in the main, the same kind of Irish Catholics that I knew from the Vennel. Unlike their counterparts in the Vennel, many of them over the years in Craigmillar had lost contact with their faith but not entirely with their Irish roots and culture.

In a city dominated by the two great opposing teams of Hibs and Hearts a surprising number of Craigmillar residents supported Glasgow Celtic, the Irish Catholic team par excellence.

I remember once meeting one of this type, that is to say a dyed-in-the-wool Celtic supporter. He was a wild man whose party trick was pulling the metal tops off beer bottles with his bare teeth. He was also a very good footballer and had graduated from playing for the local chip shop team to signing a professional contract with a famous team in the Hong Kong league, called Hong Kong Rangers. Someone once told me to ask Micky about his experience in China.

I said, "Micky, I hear you played for Hong Kong Rangers."

"Did I fuck!" he replied. "The rest of the team played for Hong Kong Rangers, ah played for Hong Kong Celtic!"

When the estate of Craigmillar was built in the sixties to solve the problem of out-of-date, slum housing, it was advanced for its time. The houses had indoor plumbing, hot running water and electricity and so it was a world away from the conditions the residents had experienced in the slums of the Cowgate.

However, it was not without its problems. The well-intentioned town planners, with, one suspects, a nod to Le Corbusier, had arranged the three- and four-storied apartment blocks with great expanses of green space in the middle. The idea was that these spaces would be used to create plots or allotments for the growing of plants and vegetables and as a contribution to self-sufficiency.

However, though this was a nice idea in theory, it was hopelessly optimistic and impractical in terms of the people concerned. These were not Highland crofting folk with horticultural skills in the blood: they were slum-dwelling urbanites who only ever engaged with a potato in one of its culinary manifestations, that is to say, roasted, fried, boiled or mashed and who would have opined, if asked what an artichoke was, that it was probably a kind of hold in wrestling.

It might have worked if the planners had provided a programme of practical help and advice to allow the residents to accommodate themselves to their high-minded aspirations for them. But they did not, and so these green spaces remained uncultivated and uncared for and ended up as dumping grounds for old prams and trolleys, bricks and cardboard boxes and all the detritus of modern urban life.

How they could have done with a People's College of Horticulture!

It is strange, but not altogether to be wondered at given the myopic nature of bureaucrats, that the town planners tried to impose their high-minded, but ultimately nonsensical ideas of self-subsistence on the uninterested and unprepared residents and, yet, failed in their primary professional duty which was to put in place the requisite logistics to make this whole new way of life possible.

They failed to foresee the need for good transport links with the rest of the city. They failed to provide the basic amenities of normal urban life. There was no plan for a cinema, a centre for health and recreation, a restaurant, a cafe or two. Above all they failed to make provision for and attract the big businesses and the quality stores that people were used to in the centre of town where they lived before. Instead, what they got were some pitifully inadequate corner shops that were as expensive as they were drab and tacky.

All of this created a feeling of isolation and disorientation that worked its evil magic for years to come and was responsible for many of the social problems that ensued. No more the cheery cry of 'Are ye in, Mary?' when they all lived cheek by jowl with each other in the old tenements. In these soulless, purpose-built estates it was best to keep yourself to yourself, to put a good lock on your door and later, when the drugs came on the scene, to park a fierce dog behind it.

Demoralisation takes many forms: it can make you acquiescent and deferential or it can make you angry and contumacious. Both of these manifested themselves in the new community of Craigmillar. There was an increase in crime, drug use and violence (in this case unmitigated) and yet these coexisted with great feelings of inadequacy and powerlessness. This struck me very forcibly on one occasion.

It was our practice, from time to time, to use the college van (a Ford transit) to take the childminded children of our trainees into the big city of Edinburgh for a day out. This was a very big deal for them, for they hardly ever left the estate.

When we set off from Craigmillar they would be singing their heads off in boisterous and truculent good humour. Then, as we passed the imaginary border of the big city, the songs would inexplicably die on their lips to be replaced by a sullen sort of silence. On the return journey they would be silent, as before, only to burst out into triumphant song when Craigmillar came into view.

There is something about that sad reminiscence that strikes me as deeply symbolic. In the People's College we were taking our trainees on that bus but giving them the confidence to sing all the way there and all the way back!

TWENTY-SIX

Part One

I was born to be a teacher as, I hope, the events of this story and my previous classroom history may confirm. But I was not to reach this Promised Land without some years in the wilderness: years of struggle, a lot of bad luck and no small number of calamities. In this respect my career mirrored, though less searingly, the history of most of my trainees in the People's College and prepared me for my work with this very vulnerable and persistently ill-omened group.

The first calamity came early.

I was coming to the end of my secondary school career when I was diagnosed with tuberculosis, following a mass screening programme at school.

I can remember very vividly the day I was given this information. Oddly enough it had little negative impact on me at the time. If anything, I felt inexplicably elated. I sat on a long, low stone wall near the school and reflected on the fact that Keats had died of this disease. This consideration made me feel somehow special, endowed, marked out, perhaps for greatness.

I was quickly disabused of these romantic notions when I arrived home and told my mother the news. She, at once, went ashen and collapsed in shock into the only armchair in the single-end flat that was our home. In my naivety, I had not realised that TB, the silent killer, was greatly dreaded at that time in the heavily populated tenements of the poor. Of course, it was a disease that struck people at all levels of society but communities, like ours, were the perfect breeding ground for this disease and it tended to go rampant in such close-knit populations.

In addition, it carried a stigma, comparable to the stigma that attached itself to Aids in a later generation. The carrier of this disease was regarded as a threat to all and became a sort of pariah, someone to be avoided at all costs.

I was blissfully unaware of this because, like so many other shocking or shameful aspects of the life of the desperately poor, it was never spoken about openly, and certainly not in the presence of children. Nevertheless, my mother's reaction to my news soon opened my eyes to the seriousness of my predicament.

In the event, the medical authorities, because it was established that I was lucky enough not to be at that stage infectious to others, gave their permission for me to remain at school for the remaining two months so that I might be able to sit my final exams, the Highers as they were called.

I passed my Highers with the bare minimum of passes that would guarantee me entrance to the university. This was my mother's burning passion and one in which I readily acquiesced, as much to please her as anything else.

As soon as I finished school I was sent to a sanatorium on the outskirts of Glasgow where I spent the next eleven months.

Being an isolation unit, no visits of friends or family were permitted. I should have hated it: a young man of seventeen just starting out in life and yet stuck in an isolation hospital for an indefinite period with nothing to do but watch my fellow patients die of a wasting and terminal disease.

In fact, the reverse was true. I remember it only for the positive aspects of the experience.

For one thing I was lodged for the duration of my stay in Blawarthill in a three-sided hut, called, somewhat pretentiously, a chalet, in the hospital grounds. Thus, I had privacy when I needed it and plenty of access to fresh air that was the basic remedy for this disease. At the same time I was able to move freely about the hospital and its spacious grounds.

The only time my freedom of movement was curtailed was during the strictly enforced siesta period in the afternoons. At this time every patient in the hospital was confined to bed, with the expectation of taking a nap (part of the treatment). During these two hours not a creature was stirring, not even a mouse, and a profound and unbroken silence descended on the whole hospital.

I say 'not a creature was stirring' but this is not strictly speaking true. In the chalet next to mine there was a man who came from my own hometown of Dumbarton and went by the name of Gun (those nicknames again) McCue. This fellow, from time to time, used to take advantage of the lightly supervised siesta time to sneak his brother into his chalet. This was against every rule in the hospital's rule book, not least because it breached the very strict isolation code.

However, my chalet-neighbour's brother did not come to visit him, as such, but to stand in or deputise for him. This was made possible because Joe, his brother, was also his identical twin. When Joe arrived at the chalet Joe would immediately jump into Gun's bed, fully dressed as he was, and cover himself with a sheet up to his neck in order to pass himself off as his twin. This was spoiled only a little by the fact that Joe perpetually wore a flat cap, called locally a 'bunnet', to cover his severe alopecia. The sight of Joe lying in bed with a sheet up to his chin and wearing a bunnet must have been highly comical. But then, who would have seen it?

With Joe tucked up safely in his bed, Gun used the opportunity to escape from the hospital grounds, over a surrounding wall, and spend the two hours of siesta time in the nearby Blawarthill Arms scooping up (or, as you would say, drinking).

Joe and Gun managed this change over so adroitly that no one, not even I in the adjoining chalet, ever saw the two of them together at any one time. In fact, their pawkish roguery only came to light when it came to an end.

One day, during siesta, by the most unfortunate of coincidences, while Joe was posing as his absent twin, the resident hospital doctor chose that moment of all moments to make an unscheduled tour of the hospital. He did this in the company of the matron, a proverbially stern hardliner. The doctor was an old buffer who with his jolly air of casual indifference gave the impression of being an ex-army doctor. This was reinforced by the jaunty manner in which he characteristically carried his walking stick under his arm.

When he reached Gun's chalet on this occasion, perceiving that the patient was awake, he called out, in an almost braying voice:

"How are you doing, McCue? Top hole, eh what?"

Joe replied, perfectly honestly, that he was very well, thank you, Doctor.

Satisfied with that, the old buffer moved on, crying, "Keep up the good work, McCue, keep up the good work!" as he cheerily waved his stick in farewell.

Now, of course, the matron who stood by the doctor's side throughout the encounter, the Wicked Stepmother to his Falstaff, was not fooled by the charade and grasped instantly what was going on. However, it was more than her job was worth to bring the matter to a head right there in front of the doctor. This would have reflected very badly on her supervisory capacity and basic patient care. So, she kept her mouth severely shut during the conversation at the chalet.

Of course, the situation never arose again for the matron put paid abruptly to the whole farce as soon as the doctor had left and Gun had condescended to return from the pub.

It was only at this point that the whole affair came to light.

It gave all of us patients a great laugh. To a man, we admired Gun's ingenuity and pluck in carrying out what was in the circumstances a tricky and bold deception. We felt, I suppose, the same delight as inmates of a prisoner-of-war camp experience when one of their number manages to make good his escape from the camp. Like they would, we mustered a cheer for Gun when he returned, chastened, to the camp on his subsequent 'recapture'.

Getting back to my own problems, I used the adjoining men's ward, which held about twenty patients, for meals, toilet and washing facilities and, of course, company. I was amazed that these people, some of them almost skeletons, could have such good humour as they displayed.

Because I was ambulant, I was able to do things for them and this gave my life a sense of purpose as well as contributing to the camaraderie that I found so uplifting in that sad place.

There were two particular patients, on opposite sides of the ward, who were continually baiting each other, banteringly, across the ward. One was Wullie McClure, a veteran of the shipyards, who was hard-bitten and coarse, both in features and in language. The other I knew only as Winton, which sounds like a surname but was the only name Wullie used in his slanging matches with him.

Winton was a young man, in his early thirties, I would guess. He looked like a refined spectre, with his delicate features and long hair that flopped languidly over one half of his face. But, for all his cultured appearance, Winton was well capable of giving as good as he got in the heated exchanges between the pair, even when they became foul-mouthed and savage, as they often did.

On one occasion I remember Wullie begging me, after one insult too many from Winton, to carry him over to Winton's bed so that he could give him a punch on the mouth. The sad fact is that I could have done so quite easily for this once-powerful man was reduced to mere skin and bone. In fact, I could have managed it using only one hand, if the truth be told. Of course, I didn't do so and the normally good relations between the pair were soon perfectly restored.

I cannot tell you how much everyone relished these verbal spats between Wullie and Winton. They were the only form of entertainment that was available to us on the ward in those days before television and were very sorely missed when, first Winton died and then, not long after, Wullie joined him in Heaven, where, no doubt, they are still knocking spots off each other to the delight of the angelic host. As far as we on Earth were concerned, their going cast a pall over all of us for a long time afterwards. It was as if someone had switched off all the lights. It took a long time to get used to the quiet of the dark. It's true what they say, isn't it, that you only miss the water when the well runs dry?

Eventually, the doctors judged that it would better serve my interests if I were to continue my recuperation at home, taking the pills (that had just been discovered as a cure for this terrible disease) and protected from further exposure to infection in hospital.

After a relatively brief period of joy and exhilaration at being back in the bosom of my loving family, my life settled down into a humdrum pattern of boring inactivity in recuperation. Unlike the great Coleridge, of whom Wordsworth said, admiringly, that 'it was good for him to be alone', I did not take well to the longueurs of enforced semi-isolation.

Deprived of the companionship of my erstwhile buddies in the sanatorium and out of touch with my former school friends who had moved on with their lives, I was left pretty much on my own – and I didn't like it. To pass the time (and that's all it was) I would go to the cinema in the middle of the day, like some gentleman of leisure, or some pathetic weirdo, more like. I would take long solitary walks along the Clyde seashore or in the hills above Dumbarton or play putting on my own in the deserted putting green in the Public Park.

It was not easy for me to make new friends at this point, due to the stigma that I have already mentioned was attached to this illness. The demanded degree of self-distancing was as much on my part as theirs and was done very discreetly. You wouldn't have known it was happening unless you were at the centre of it.

This applied very much to my relations with the opposite sex. I was at that time very ill at ease and shy anyway in the company of girls. This resulted, largely, from the fact that, except for an initial period in the 'baby class' of the wonderful Sister Gertrude, I had spent my entire

221

scholastic career in all-boys' classes (not uncommon in the state Catholic sector). This shyness in the presence of girls went toxic when allied to the restraints put upon me by my diagnosed tuberculosis. Thus, I was deprived of the consolation of female company also at this critical point in my isolation.

You would have thought that I could have made friends with my fellow afflicted in the area (for misery, as they say, loves company). But this was not so. Because of that terrible working-class reticence about bad news, I simply did not know of any people of a similar age to myself who suffered from this illness.

Furthermore, the only time fellow sufferers, like myself, met up was at the mass check-ups, which were held every three months or so. These occasions were in no way conducive to establishing relationships among the patients. This was because of the almost brutal manner in which they were conducted.

The chief medical officer of health for the county and his team of doctors would travel to selected venues in the county to conduct mass check-up events. There were only two sessions to this one-day event: one starting at eight o'clock in the morning and one at two o'clock in the afternoon. Because my surname is in the latter half of the alphabet I was always summoned to the two o'clock slot (and seldom got out much before six).

The first time I turned up for my 'appointment' at the waiting room provided, I thought that I had stumbled upon a mass sit-in or protest of some kind. The waiting room, that looked like a converted drill hall, was filled wall to wall with benches which were occupied by close-packed people of all ages. There must have been eighty to a hundred of them in the room.

There was no appointment system as such. It was a strictly first-come, first-serve basis. The waiting people simply shuffled along the benches and down the rows, like modern-day airport passengers, until it was their turn to be seen by the doctor. The possibilities of communication were limited to the people on either side of you and usually they would be people who had little in common with each other or with you.

But, apart from the unsophisticated (to put it mildly) appointment system and some humiliating elements in the whole process, what impressed me most about these claustrophobic sessions was the surprising discovery of just how many people of all ages in the local and national population were victims of this disease. I had no idea, till then, of the magnitude of what I had got myself into.

Part Two

Fortunately, throughout my time at the sanatorium and subsequently, I had remained non-infectious to others and the day eventually arrived when the county medical team gave me permission to take up the course on offer to me at Glasgow University.

I became an undergraduate in the arts faculty, studying in my first year English, History and Latin.

Right from the start I knew that this was a mistake. Whether it was due to the long break in my studies or some more deep-seated inadequacy on my part, I cannot say, but I was all at sea. I had no proper study habits and these were vitally necessary for the manner in which an arts MA was conducted at that time, in Glasgow at least.

The stars of the department, usually the professor himself, would deliver lectures, mostly based on one of their published works, and the students would take notes. There was no opportunity to question or interrogate the material. As for everything else, you were left to get on with it as best you could.

I am not saying that this method in itself was in any way flawed or inadequate. After all, it had served generations of Scottish students well over the centuries. The slightest acquaintance with the eighteenth-century novelists will testify that the reputation for learning of the Scottish graduates that travelled to London at that time was extremely high.

However engrossing and even brilliant these lectures were in the hands of a master, they were, in a sense, a sideshow. The real work took place in the library and in private study: reading everything in sight; novels, poetry, plays, works of criticism, biographies, and, if you were really keen, learned articles. This was a lonely job and took strong motivation and good study habits. I had neither and so did less and less work and fell further and further behind.

The final straw came when I handed in my first Latin assignment in early December. Though at school I had been the best in my class at Latin, I seemed to have forgotten, in the meantime, everything I once knew. My grasp of the intricacies of Latin grammar was highly approximate, to say the most. Small wonder, then, that the examiner should say of that first assignment of mine that 'it was not like a language at all, but a collection of primitive sounds'.

Time to go! I thought. *The game's up!*

I did not formally resign from my degree course. With typical fecklessness, I simply stopped going. Nor did I, at first, tell my mother. I just stayed out of her way and let her think that everything was all right.

Until it wasn't!

Eventually I had to face the fact that I could no longer pretend that I was a student and, so, would have to find myself a job. This was an unbelievably difficult thing for me to contemplate. I had no idea where I could find work or what I would be capable of doing. The idea of looking for a job simply horrified me.

Luckily, at this point, fate took a hand and on the basis of my MA Glasgow (Failed) and the kind services of a friend of the family who worked there in a senior capacity, I got a job in a large optical firm in the district. And not just any job. But the job of trainee manager, if you please!

To say I was delighted would be a great understatement. I was ecstatic! I had something pridefully to offer my mother to compensate for the collapse of her ambition to produce the first graduate in our family's history. At no effort on my part I was in a post that commanded respect. I was managerial material!

This seemingly wonderful opportunity soon turned out to be merely a false dawn and ended ignominiously.

As part of my training in the job, I was put into the dispatch department to learn the ropes. The head of department was so good at her job that she found it difficult, if not impossible, to delegate, especially to the blundering novice that I was at that time. I found myself with less and less to do. That little I was given was repetitive and dull and so I was afforded no opportunity to flourish or show my real potential to senior management.

At the same time I was in that angry socialist phase that the young often go through on their way to becoming outrageously right wing in their later years (I never did). I was at that time what the Italians call a *cattocomunista*, that is to say, someone who is a devout Catholic in religion (I attended early morning Mass before work every day) and a fervent communist in politics.

I delighted in going through the factory whistling communist songs, like 'La Bandiera Rossa' and the 'Internationale', to wind up the management and my colleagues on the staff who were all to a man fierce anti-communists, as was quite common in that period of the Cold War.

Then something happened that was in no way my fault but which had disastrous consequences for me.

The workers in the factory went on strike and forced the management into a humiliating capitulation. The nub of the dispute and its eventual resolution centred on critical production figures that had fallen into the hands of the Union that the company could not afford to be made public.

The strike was settled on the usual mutually accepted basis of 'no victimisation'. Except that there was a victim.

And it was me! And I wasn't even a member of the Union (this was forbidden to staff).

I was sent for and accused of passing the data in question on to the union. This was based upon the fact that I was doing my training in the dispatch department and, so, had, theoretically, access to the production figures. In answer to this I said that if someone had stopped me in Dumbarton High Street and asked me the weekly total of lenses we were producing and if, by some miracle, I actually knew the answer, I would have revealed it unhesitatingly, since I did not see why the number of lenses they were making per week should be kept a secret from the people who actually made them. However, I added, strictly for the record: I did not have that figure at my fingertips, nobody asked the question and so, therefore, I could not and did not divulge the information to anyone.

After making insultingly short work of all other possible suspects (the secretary who typed the data in the first place was dismissed as 'just a silly bitch') and despite my protest of total innocence, I was summarily dismissed on the charge, no less, of 'industrial espionage'. In the act of dismissing me, the chief executive gestured languidly in the direction of the low-lying Kilpatrick hills and intoned, "I fully believe, McLaughlin, that at the weekends you are in those hills in radio contact with Moscow."

Distraught at the false accusation and its inevitable consequences, I went immediately to the shop steward of the Union who was by this time a good friend of mine (amongst other things I played for the factory football team) and explained everything. Bunger, for that was his nickname, immediately offered to clear my name, even at the cost of losing a vital bargaining chip in his later dealings with the management. I refused to let him do so, for, as he and I both knew, the management had no love for me and would seek the earliest opportunity to get rid of me, especially now.

Bunger, who had been an old friend of my father's, trusted me enough to tell me how he had come upon the information that won the strike for the Union. It was banal in the extreme.

One Friday evening as he and the other workers were going over the bridge to their homes in the nearby village of Renton he fell into step with a colleague who was the firm's lorry driver. This man's job comprised spending one whole week unloading, at destination after destination, the lenses produced in our factory all the way down to the south of England and picking up essential raw materials on the way back. Though he looked like and considered himself to be an ordinary worker, the company had insisted on making him a member of staff, and, therefore, non-unionised, because of the sensitivity and importance of his role and their paranoia about security and secrecy.

Anyway, as he and Bunger conversed on their way across the bridge he complained bitterly, as workers will do, about the stresses of his job and, in particular, about the extremely heavy loads he was having to carry at that time. To reinforce his complaint and to elicit the appropriate degree of sympathy he actually specified the exact number of lenses he had carried that week, down to a single lens. Bunger couldn't believe his good luck.

This figure proved conclusively what he had suspected all along, namely that our firm was boosting production (the furnaces were going night and day and the overtime was plentiful) in some sort of Masters' Federation Agreement or capitalist conspiracy involving a rival optical firm in England whose workers, we knew, were out on strike at that time. Our firm was obviously supplying this, supposedly rival, firm with enough lenses to keep their orders going and thus, effectively beat the strike. Amongst other things this behaviour carried the faint whiff of commercial fraud.

It was intolerable that workers in Scotland should be working overtime in order to keep fellow trade unionists in England out of a job. It breached every principle of the brotherhood of labour. When Bunger heard this precise figure he knew immediately that he had the management over a barrel. It was all he could do to keep a straight face. He kept repeating the figure silently to himself to keep it fresh in his mind. The moment they arrived in the pub, the first port of call for the workers on a Friday night, he excused himself to go to the toilet. Once there, he wrote the precise figure on the back of a cigarette packet before he could forget it.

The rest played out as I have described it. The workers, at Bunger's behest, rather than go on outright strike as they initially wished to do, simply banned all overtime in our factory. This had the effect of making it very difficult for our firm to meet their own obligations, far less buoy up their competitor-friends.

The intimidating factor had been the precision of the output figures, which Bunger claimed had come from the exceptionally well-informed and ubiquitous investigation branch of the Union. This threat would be enough to keep the management straight and would continue to hang over them for the foreseeable future. This is why he was loath to give it up even to clear me. Needless to say there was no such investigative section in the upper echelons of the union, but it was credible and that was good enough for Bunger – and, apparently, for the management of the firm.

They say that for the want of a shoe the battle was lost: this battle would have been lost if Bunger hadn't had a pencil handy that night in the pub.

Being, again, unemployed posed great problems for me but if I had to leave a job, doing so with the designation of spy was not the least satisfactory of outcomes. At least it fed my romantic ego.

Part Three

I managed to find myself a menial clerical post in an engineering firm in the area. The work was mind-numbingly boring and tedious. In desperation at the dullness and terrible greyness of my life as a junior clerk, on impulse, I attended an audition in Edinburgh organised by a showbusiness impresario who was recruiting acts for his network of summer shows. I passed the audition and soon found myself as lead singer and second top of the bill in a variety show in the north of England. This is not as surprising as it may at first sight appear for I had done some work in public as an amateur soloist, singing art songs and light opera. In the show I was publicly billed as 'The Connemara Orphan' and this was pretty bizarre because I was neither Irish nor an orphan and the only clothes I had to wear in my act were the white tie and tails full evening wear that I had purchased in a local pawnshop and wore in my previous capacity as a concert singer. I was supposed to be a poor Irish orphan but I appeared on stage looking like some matinee idol. Say Jack Buchanan or Fred Astaire. Still the audience loved it and I was quite a success. I began to dream, like some pathetic Hollywood hopeful, of a career in show business with the fame and fortune that would surely go with it.

Sadly, it was not to be. At this point my life took another surprising turn, sideways this time.

Someone who had been a notable principal singer with the Carl Rosa Opera Company, and whom I had never met, caught my act and wrote to Sadler's Wells Opera, one of the two most prestigious opera companies in Great Britain, recommending me to their attention. The possibility of a career in opera trumped show business and then some so I went down to London, as summoned, and auditioned for Sadler's Wells.

They did not take me on right away, partly on account of my youth and partly on account of my lack of professional training but they did pay for me to take operatic singing lessons at the Royal Scottish Academy of Music and Drama in Glasgow where, though I was only a part-timer,

I was awarded, in the teeth of some fierce competition, the principal role of Aeneas in the academy's end-of-term production of Handel's opera, *Dido and Aeneas*.

This was the high point of my career as a singer and the moment of greatest triumph in my life to this point. Yet, in the end, it was important for what it led to, rather than what it was.

It was at this exciting moment in my life that I had an epiphany moment.

I suddenly realised with astonishing clarity that, though I was a good singer, even, demonstrably, a very good singer, I knew in my heart that I would never be a great one. I visualised myself in a room full of really great singers and realised that in such a room I would count for little, if anything. The thought did not appeal to me; indeed it chilled me to the marrow. It suited my personality to imagine myself in a room full of my peers, even in some less rarified sphere, where I could look everyone in the eye and say, "I am as good as anyone in this room."

For some reason I can't explain, I thought that I could do that as a teacher. I had been inspired by many teachers I had known in my childhood, like Tommy O'Donnell, my old history teacher at secondary school, and the redoubtable Andy Powell, that colossus from Kerry that I have already told you about. Much as I admired them and looked up to them, I did not lack the confidence that I could emulate them. Heady thought!

I immediately left music school and my part in the opera and arranged to go back to university to resume the degree course that I had so cavalierly abandoned some years before. This would pave my way to becoming a teacher.

As usual with me, nothing was as simple as it appeared to be. Right there, with my boats already burnt, I faced a major stumbling block. Because I had left university that first time without informing the university authorities of my decision, I was deemed to have completed the first year of the degree course. In order to proceed into what would be, according to the rules, my second year, and this was my only option, I would have to pass the degree level exam in one of my original subjects.

How could I possibly do this? I did not have a scrap of paper from my previous attempt and not even the haziest memories of anything I was exposed to in the couple of months of my purported attendance. I had no contacts with the university, was an outsider, friendless and alone.

There was only one course open to me – and it was a desperate one. I must create a university course for myself in one of my original subjects and then pass the exam on the basis of it!

To choose Latin was out of the question for obvious reasons, and though I was naturally good at English, I thought that the subject might present unexpected problems in terms of course construction and rubrics. So, I opted for history. History, I reasoned, was safe enough; if you knew all the facts and dates and could write well and analytically what could be the problem?

To cut a long story short, in order to support myself, I was working at the time in the massive Singer's Sewing

Machine factory in Clydebank, inevitably as a junior clerk, my level at the time. I took to spending every lunch hour in the exclusively reference section of the Clydebank Public Library frantically making copious notes from the massive volumes of the *Cambridge World History* for the relevant period of my interest. This was the only book I consulted but it was famously comprehensive and authoritative and I thought that it would serve the purpose.

For months on end, I read and read this massive tome, without ceasing, and took notes till my fingers ached. I suppose that it was a very brutal and amateurish way of going about things. But it worked!

However, not before fate played one last dastardly trick on me.

When I turned up at the university at the appointed time to sit the exam I had so assiduously prepared for, I found a crowd of young undergraduates clustered excitedly in groups just outside the door of the examination hall. I felt very detached from this hubbub of young eager beavers. I was a bag of nerves, well outside my comfort zone. I doubted everything. Most of all myself and, even, my right to be there.

In need of reassurance and in panic I asked a young fellow who stood near me, "This is the right place for History Three, isn't it?"

"No, pal, never heard of History Three. This is the queue for History B."

He turned to one of his companions and said, "That's right, isn't it, there's no History Three, is there?"

His companion replied, "Not now, there isn't. There used to be years ago. My big brother took it but it doesn't exist now."

The bastards had changed the course! I was, as they say in Glasgow, up the River Clyde without a paddle. All those hours of agony in the Clydebank Public Library had gone for nothing. It had all been a complete waste of time and effort.

At that moment the servitor opened the doors of the examination hall and all the students began excitedly pouring in. In panic I pushed my way, brusquely, through the crowd and grabbed the servitor by the lapels and screamed, "History Three! History Three!"

He pushed me back gently and said, somewhat pityingly, "Get a grip, my lad! Go straight through the main examination hall and you will find the room for resits of History Three."

I did as he said and found myself in a little side room with five or six others looking as abject as I was feeling at the time.

A sympathetic invigilator approached me and said, "You're lucky, you know. When the university changes a course, they are bound by the regulations to offer it for a period of three successive years to former candidates. That period is up now and this is the very last opportunity for anyone to resit this exam. Good luck!"

Whether the authorities had compassionately decided to make it as easy as possible for the maximum number to pass on this historic final occasion or whether my preparations had been even more thorough than I imagined, I do not know. Suffice to say the exam seemed perfectly straightforward and I passed it with ease, I think. Either way, I passed it and that was the only thing that mattered.

So, once again, I found myself back in the university fold. Only this time I was greatly changed. The setbacks I had experienced in life had toughened me up and maturity had given me a practicality which my former self could never have dreamed of. I became renowned in the class for my work rate and vast reading and passed all my subsequent exams with greater and greater ease till I emerged from the university with an Honours MA in English Language and Literature. Thereafter I attended the Jordanhill College of Education and acquired my teaching diploma.

And this is where we found ourselves at the very beginning of this story: back at the school I attended as a boy and on the threshold of a career that would lead, ultimately, to the People's College.

Like my students in Craigmillar, I had, by determination, some desperation and not a little luck, successfully negotiated a difficult path, strewn with boulders and pitfalls, to achieve success in life and work.

This was the sort of success that now awaited my trainees after all their travails before and during their time with us.

It is to record this success that I happily turn in the next chapter.

TWENTY-SEVEN

This is the happy part of the story when we get the opportunity to recount the success of our efforts to get our former hopeless cases into work, with the promise of a stable and more fulfilling life ahead of them.

Our success rate, at 85%, was, of course, very high and certainly high enough to guarantee, with ease, our continued funding by Europe. But, I admit, it did not entirely sit well with me.

After all, translated into actual numbers of individuals – and individuals were always our focus – it meant that four people out of every thirty in our normal intake did not get into work straight after completion of the course. This would have seemed unacceptably high to me if it were not for the fact that it did not tell the whole story.

According to the strict rules of our funding, a successful outcome was based on two criteria: either the individual was in a permanent job by a month after leaving the course, or was enrolled in full-time, further education.

Sometimes the job came along – and with our help – but only after the qualifying period had expired. This was not entirely uncommon due to the way our training operated. We were setting out to produce individuals who would have strong personal resources and motivation and so would be able to act autonomously, without the constant need of a helping hand on the back. So, we were quite relaxed about finding them a job and if it came, on a small number of occasions, too late to be included in our success statistics, so be it. With us, it was always the big picture that counted.

Besides, due to the nature of our establishment, the college was always there, available to them on a casual basis, even after their official funding had ceased. This was the great merit of creating our own college to provide the training. Though it was just some rooms in a large, multi-occupancy art deco building, it had acquired status and solidity through the regular and successive intakes and came to be perceived as a genuine seat of learning, albeit on a small scale.

This sense of continuity and endurance through time meant that the People's College became a reference point for former trainees, who frequently came to visit us, tell of their progress and seek, where necessary, concrete help or advice. We also provided, gratuitously, a mentoring service for ex-trainees faced with the necessity of acquiring some specific qualification not covered in our curriculum. You will see a good example of this when I come to talk about our connections with the fire brigade.

All in all, we were a proper little, old-fashioned alma mater set in the improbable wilds of uncultivated Craigmillar.

But there were other ways that an apparent failure could mask a thoroughgoing success. I will quote the case of young Tom Devanney.

Tom was an only child who had been forced to leave school early to nurse his mother when she developed cancer. When she died two years later, Tom's life went into a tailspin and he began to drink to excess and even dabbled in drugs for a while.

With the help of a strong religious sense, he managed to put his life in order and found his way to our door. In the course of his time with us – and I am not claiming here any causal factor in this – he discovered a religious vocation and, after completing his full course with us he left to join a religious order as a brother.

Of course, this did not qualify as a permanent job under the rules and could not count in our statistics but when I tell you what happened to Tom subsequently I will leave it to you to judge whether he was a success or not and whether or not we had any role in it.

After many years of dedication and patient study Tom became a priest and, when last heard of, was working in a poor parish in the Archdiocese of Edinburgh and Saint Andrew's where he is greatly loved for his down-to-earth good nature and for his fatherly compassion, particularly in the confessional.

Tom reminds me very much of a curate we had in our parish of Saint Patrick's in Dumbarton when I was a young boy growing up.

Father O'Callaghan was a dynamic and outgoing young Irish priest. He was very popular, not least because he was a man's man par excellence. Father O'Callaghan, when confronting a would-be hardman who was beating his wife, had been known to offer to take his collar off. This is the equivalent of a man removing his jacket in preparation for a fight. It was never ineffective and many's the abused wife had good reason to bless dear Father O'Callaghan for finally putting an end to her abuse.

Father O'Callaghan's robust Christianity puts me in mind of a repeated saying of my own father who, as we have seen, was a noted pugilist in the area. After yet one more lecture from my mother on the subject of his lack of fervour in performing his spiritual duties, my father would reply, "Look, Mary, there are three kinds of Catholics: the praying Catholics, the paying Catholics and the fighting Catholics. I'm a member of the Church Militant and, as such, I am always ready to take my jacket off for the Pope."

As well as being very amiable and good-natured, except when roused to righteous indignation, Father O'Callaghan had a puckish sense of humour and this is demonstrated to good effect in the little anecdote which follows.

After his curacy in Dumbarton came to an end, Father O'Callaghan was moved to Glasgow to become parish priest in the church of Our Lady of Lourdes in Cardonald in a poor area of the city.

At that time in one of the leafy suburbs of the city there was a parish called Christ the King. The parish priest of this affluent church was much advanced in years. A convert from Anglicanism, he had risen to become an auxiliary bishop in the Roman Catholic Archdiocese of Glasgow. Bishop Martin was very much aware of his dignity and his aristocratic origins and, when answering the phone would characteristically exclaim in his lofty, English tones:

"Chra-ist the King here!"

One day Fr O'Callaghan had occasion to phone Bishop Martin.

The old bishop answered with his usual pomposity, "Chra-ist the King here!"

Fr O'Callaghan responded tartly, "It's yer mammy, son. Our Lady of Lourdes!"

Of course, our small degree of failure, that bothered nobody but ourselves, could not in the real world be avoided. Like death and taxes, it was inevitable. Being eminently practical people we just put our disappointments aside and got on with the day job. There was so much to do and be uplifted by; for example the successes achieved by our trainees.

For the males in our midst the outcomes achieved were largely predictable. They were in such things as industry and the building trade. Two young men, in widely differing intakes, managed to obtain posts in the fire brigade. Not as easy as you might think. When I went to investigate the possibility of getting someone into the fire brigade college, I discovered that there was an exam to pass and it seemed to me surprisingly stiff.

The expectations of the Maths and English sections were unexpectedly high. This gave me an entirely new respect for firefighters, who I now saw, not only as plucky and resourceful individuals, but also as veritable Renaissance men in their accomplishments.

After a programme of specific tutoring on our part, our two trainees managed to pass the entrance exam for the fire brigade college and so go on to have careers as firefighters.

Only one male trainee to my knowledge went into retail but he was an interesting case.

When Tom Barrett came to us he was in the throes of despair. He had been cruelly made redundant at the age of fifty, after a lifetime in one particular firm. Because of his age he was finding it impossible to interest potential employers.

Tom was a spry and smartly dressed individual who was impeccably polite and easy-going. Being much older than the rest, he soon became the father of the class and a great influence on the younger ones.

In his coursework he was marvellously enthusiastic. He took to Cosmology with great enthusiasm and adored Creative Writing where his greater experience of life came into its own.

With our help he got a placement and then a job in one of the big department stores in Edinburgh. He ended up as manager of the white goods department where his very dapper appearance and his genteel manners proved a great asset.

Amongst the women, the range of successful outcomes was much wider than it was for the men.

Some got jobs in administration; for example in a school office or in the office of a housing association, or even in the council offices, though this was, for the most part, discouraged as being slightly iffy, due to the council's role in our funding. We put this down to mere moral scruples and did not stand in the way when a job with the council came the way of any of our trainees. After all, this was never likely to come to the attention of our European funders and, as for the council, they just winked a conspiratorial eye.

A considerable number of jobs acquired by our female trainees was in the general field of care. Thus we had a few who made a career out of care of the elderly. This was before the sector was taken over by the fly-by-night capitalists with their squeezed-for-profit budgets, zero-hours contracts and all the other tricks of their modern nefarious trade.

A good number became classroom assistants. Where someone found a particular opening it was often the case that others followed her through the breach.

Retail was also a sector in which many of the female trainees found a career. This was almost always in the city centre. Retail was a world we had opened to them through our ambitious placement-seeking skills, a world in which, amongst other things, their natural talents for easy sociability flourished. Easy sociability was a talent more characteristic of friendly Glasgow than frosty Edinburgh, but our Craigmillar trainees came as close to that affable Glasgow ideal as you could get in the east of Scotland.

Some jobs we found for our female trainees were more one-off and exotic. I remember the case of Bernadette. Bernadette was a very striking-looking young woman with long blonde hair. She was the only girl in a family of four brothers and was a bit of a tomboy. She was passionately interested in motorcars and was known as a highly skilled driver. So much so in fact that it was rumoured that on occasion she had acted as getaway driver for some gangland associates when they were engaged in illicit activities. I heard the story but didn't fall for that Bonnie and Clyde nonsense for a moment. The people of Craigmillar are great fantasists and love nothing more than a good story. In fact I suspect that the rumour was put about by Bernadette herself to gain some added street cred and glamour.

We found the ideal placement for her with a quality car hire firm which dealt only with luxury limousines for a very select clientele. On the basis of her looks and her driving skills it seemed the perfect match. And indeed it was! She went on to get a permanent job with the company and became a great success as chauffeuse to the rich.

Years later it was reported to me that she subsequently married the owner of the franchise and is now driven around in the top-of-the-range limousines that she was once paid to drive for others. I took that story with more than a pinch of salt. It smacks of Fantasy Island, if you ask me.

As you might expect, given the scholastic structure of the People's College, a good number of our trainees went into further education after the course. The most interesting representative of this group was Frank Folan.

Frank had come to us with a Higher art qualification acquired at school before he succumbed to problems with drink and bad company. When he joined us he was very nervous about the whole college thing mainly on account of the fact that he was incurably shy and insecure. In the event he coped well and became very popular, particularly on account of his ability as a skilled artist. During the lunch hour he would make pencil sketches of the trainees, particularly the female trainees, which were highly prized for their accuracy and, often, subtle humour.

It was during Frank's period with us that I had the idea of producing a college newsletter that we would distribute to every house in Craigmillar, as well as to outside interested bodies like the Edinburgh Council, partners and the local and professional press.

We gave the job of designing this newsletter to Frank. And what a wonderful job he made of it!

The masthead he designed was simply brilliant, both in concept and execution. He picked out the letters of our title, *The Collegian*, as if they were rough-hewn and uneven monoliths. He wittily included a miniscule cartoon figure of himself as a Stone-Age man putting the finishing touches to the letter 'n' with an anachronistic hammer and chisel. He perfectly captured in the rough-hewn stones the down-to-earth nature of our origins as well as our sense of building something that would last.

It was partly also a little joke at our own expense. Recognising this, the *Times Educational Supplement*, in a complimentary little piece on our newsletter, said that the title made the People's College seem like a small preparatory school for privileged rich kids somewhere in Vermont.

Frank went on, after completing his time with us, to train in cartoon and animation design in Dundee and eventually found work in that area which has subsequently become famous as the Silicon Valley of this specialism.

An unlooked-for outcome which came our way was the number of our trainees who subsequently showed entrepreneurial talent. I will take as an example of this group Bridget, the 'Fur Finisher', that you will remember from a previous encounter. We found Bridget a placement and then a permanent job with a large office-cleaning firm.

After getting as much as she could from this experience, Bridget had the idea of going into business for herself. She saw a gap in the market and with two colleagues, also ex-trainees, she set up a cleaning business of her own, servicing the holiday-home letting trade. Now, many years later, she makes a good living for herself and her family because the holiday-home lets and Airbnb sector has greatly expanded in tourist-rich Edinburgh and in the picturesque little towns of East Lothian that lie in its vicinity.

You remember Marilyn whose high-profile past as a shoplifter supreme and a heavy drug-user I recounted earlier? Well, Marilyn got a job in, of all places, a chemist shop. And not just anywhere, but in Craigmillar itself. She was so successful in this job that she was swiftly promoted to head assistant in the pharmacy section, as far as she could go without a degree.

The fact that she was given this post at all says a great deal for the magnanimity of her employers, for they knew her past perfectly well. It also testifies to Marilyn's own strength of character and resolution for she must have come in for a great deal of pressure from addicts in the area that she had known in the past. Still, she saw it all through and now is a stalwart of the community and respected by all.

Now I come to the case of Mohammed and Fatima, our immigrant doctors, who, as you will remember, were refused permission to start the process of being recognised as doctors in the UK as a result of Cold War politics.

Well, both had extremely successful outcomes as a direct result of our efforts, though not specifically as a result of our training programme.

Recognising that the greatest, indeed the only, impediment to their getting into work in Britain was the political block on the acceptance of their qualifications, we set out to change the mind of the government on this issue. Such was our confidence in our own ability (or sheer chutzpah, if you must) that there wasn't a windmill we weren't ready to have a tilt at.

Right there in our humble little base of the People's College we mounted a campaign to this effect. We lobbied everyone in sight: local politicians, the national political parties, civil liberties groups, the Commonwealth Office. We even wrote to the Prime Minister at the time, John Major, whose response to our letter was courteous, sympathetic but, ultimately, irresolute.

Our campaign appeared to have come to nothing.

Then, one wonderful day, Mohammed and Fatima came bounding into our office joyously waving the latest edition of the *British Medical Journal* that had just arrived by post at their home. And there, plump as a pigeon, was a full-page paid announcement from the British Government declaring that as of that date all medical degrees and qualifications obtained in Bangladesh during that crucial period of two years were now fully recognised and that any such graduates were welcome to offer themselves for examination to become medical practitioners in the UK.

The UK Government had caved in!

The joy in the Unit at the news was unconfined, for, besides representing a great victory for our efforts and for justice, it secured a very happy ending for Mohammed and Fatima who were liked by all and admired for their humble and helpful demeanour in all the classes.

Both sailed through the formalities required for acceptance. Fatima almost immediately found a post as a registrar in a hospital in Leeds. Subsequently, the family moved to New Zealand where both found jobs as consultants in the New Zealand Health Service.

Though we never received any formal acknowledgement of our contribution to this volte-face on the part of the government, we were contacted by some of the organisations we had lobbied to congratulate us on our achievement.

One very senior person at the Commonwealth Office informed us that we had done much more than we could have imagined because we had, inadvertently, brought about a country-wide mini-crisis in the Indian restaurant business.

Apparently, on the same day that Mohammed and Fatima received the news, a thousand or more Bangladesh waiters and cooks abruptly left their restaurant jobs and began the process to become registered as doctors in Great Britain.

Today Craigmillar; tomorrow the world.

Now we come to the related case of Monica Odsuma, our teacher from Nigeria. You may recall that she came to us because she was unable to get a job because the Nigerian Government refused to provide the documentation necessary to prove that she was a qualified and experienced teacher.

She had fled the country, as you will remember, when, in a coup, a military regime took over. The new government out of malice at her defection refused to release her documentation.

We got in touch with the Scottish General Teaching Council, which is the body that, amongst other things, accredits the qualifications of all would-be teachers in Scotland. They were very sympathetic and became very supportive of us.

Monica's former headteacher in Nigeria turned out to be a very helpful and resourceful ally. Surprisingly so. She got in contact (how?) with subversive elements in Nigeria opposed to the new government and they arranged for an operative (let's not beat about the bush, a spy) to break into the offices of the Nigerian Education Department and microfilm all the relevant documents in Monica's file.

This film was subsequently passed through a covert chain of associates out of the country. Eventually the information arrived at the desk of the General Teaching Council. They at once ratified her qualifications. Almost immediately, she secured a post as a secondary school teacher in Hackney. We have not heard of her since.

It is a case that puzzles me still. When I reflect on the extraordinary lengths these subversive elements in Nigeria went to in order to get a simple schoolteacher a job in a foreign country, I wonder if Monica was quite the wide-eyed innocent she purported to be or, rather, someone altogether more important in the world of Nigerian politics.

We'll never know.

In any case, what does it matter?

The final happy ending I wish to record is the case of John Irvine (not his real name), the failed businessman that I told you about earlier in this story who had been cheated out of his business by a corrupt and unscrupulous partner. Well, with our encouragement and inspired by our creative writing programme he subsequently wrote a book charting the rise and fall of his business which enjoyed a notable degree of success. More importantly, it led to him making a decent career for himself as an acclaimed and scintillating after-dinner speaker at business events and venues up and down the country.

Maybe Creative Writing wasn't the only part of our whole educational package that inspired him, if the title he chose to give his book is anything to go by. He called it *To the Stars and Back: A Cautionary Tale*.

As for 'Happy Feet' MacCorkindale, our bankrupt ex-footballer, he has made a decent career for himself organising football tournaments for the indigent and the unemployed.

TWENTY-EIGHT

Now we come to consider the wider impact the People's College had in the community and beyond.

We will start, in Yeats' words, where 'all our ladders start, in the foul rag-and-bone shop of the heart', that is, in the lives of our own little community in the People's College.

Certainly, as we have seen, we found jobs for them, and good jobs too, but much more important and long-lasting was the transformative effect of our programme on the lives and perspectives of our trainees. Lives were changed, and forever.

You remember Maggie Broon who came to realise that she was in every sense a star?

She was not the only one. Almost all of our trainees on completion of the course felt themselves enhanced, souped up. They felt as if they were taking giant, ten-metre strides in a gravity-free atmosphere, instead of struggling, sluggishly, through the sea of thick molasses that was their former, deprived reality.

The psychological transformation that took place in our trainees, almost from the first, was evident to any visitor. Their very faces radiated confidence and contentment.

In no single individual was this transformative power more evident than it was in the case of George McGuigan.

George was in our very first batch of students and was almost a metaphor for disadvantage. He was no great physical specimen. He was slight in build and moved in a characteristically jerky and nervous manner that made him seem perpetually deferential. He came from a notorious family that was much despised locally as petty thieves and troublemakers. Nor was their bad reputation limited to the local area of Craigmillar. The whole family and every individual in it was barred from even entering most of the pubs in the centre of Edinburgh. In fact, George and his family had all the hallmarks of being originally of traveller or gypsy stock and had been brought low by constant revulsion and prejudice to the condition of outsiders.

Certainly, George had the look of a social outcast when I first set eyes on him. He was pitiful in many respects. His clothes, though clean enough, were none of the best. He had a pinched or malnourished look. He looked like the sort of spectre you might find wandering alone and lost in a field of battle after the conflict has ended. His school education had been a disaster, that is when he deigned to attend at all.

All in all, he did not appear very prepossessing as a candidate for the People's College. Or, come to think about it, maybe he did.

Oddly enough, I have absolutely no memory of choosing George. I rather think that George chose us. Either that or Lizzie, our secretary, chose him for she had always been fond of George.

And, in truth, as we soon discovered, George was easy to like.

He was perpetually good-natured and cheery and terribly willing. He was always volunteering for things, like that Corporal Jones in the sitcom, *Dad's Army*.

We had put up a series of posters round the office in our early days that were meant to be challenging or uplifting. One was from Goethe: 'Grey is all theory; green grows the golden tree of life'. Another one was of my own making (I think). It said: 'Every person's mind is a mansion with many apartments. Most of us live in only one or two rooms, sometimes the basement. Go, open up a few more rooms in your mind. Let the sunshine in!'.

George must have been very impressed by this poster, as will emerge later, though he at no time made reference to it either to me or to anyone else on the staff.

George loved being at the People's College and everyone at the college loved George because of his great good-nature and enthusiasm. Both were shown to life-saving effect on one early occasion.

It was an important part of our total package of preparation for work that every trainee should undergo a course of first aid organised by the St John's Ambulance Brigade at their headquarters in the centre of Edinburgh.

George attended that very first course, along with the others. On their way back to the bus stop that would take them home to Craigmillar, an elderly man, a perfect stranger to them, collapsed at the bus stop in front of them as a result of a heart attack. George, at once, typically, told the others to stand back and proceeded to administer the kiss of life (that he had just learned minutes before) and, so, saved the old man's life.

It was about six weeks after this event that we celebrated the official, formal opening of the People's College.

It was a very grand event attended by senior officers of the Craigmillar Festival Society, Edinburgh City councillors and other prominent members of the community. I asked the students if any of them felt able to say a few words at the event. Naturally, George volunteered himself right away. My heart sank but I didn't have the heart to turn him down. So, in due course, George got his opportunity to speak in public for the first, and perhaps only, time in his life. And it wasn't only a few stumbling words either, so, I will relate them now, as near as I can remember them, in his own words.

"When ah first came here tae the Peeple's College," he said, "ah wis, if ye can picture it, like an auld broken doon mansion-hoose wi' the slates fawin' aff the roof an' nae gless in the windaes. At night it wis like an auld hoose in wan o' thae horror films. Noo an' again, ye wid hae seen an odd caunnel (candle) showing in a windae or two, so that it looked as if the hoose wis haunted. It wid hae scared the livin' daylights oot o' ye. Noo since ah've been here, that hoose has a light in every room. At night it's like a muckle, great lighthoose an' can be seen fur miles an' miles."

His enthusiastic self-affirmation could be perceived as an exaggeration, but, if it was not the truth as men know it, it was God's truth. George was a light, a beacon, an example, not only to his comrades-in-arms in the People's College but to all who met him in the course of his time with us. One of nature's gentlemen.

This kind of Supernova moment was not confined to people like George. Others, almost all the others, that entered our portals, had similar moments of what you might call exaltation, as out of what seemed like nothing sprang forth vibrant, confident and well-informed individuals, sparkling with life and new-found optimism.

As for the impact on the community of the sudden arrival in their midst of people that were talking, so excitedly, about the weird and wonderful things that they were doing at the People's College, it was instant and electric.

The community of Craigmillar is a tangled web of friendships, intimacies, family ties and class solidarity. If you touch the net at any point, the whole web vibrates.

And vibrate it certainly did.

Suddenly everyone was talking about the People's College. Almost everyone knew someone who was a student there or had been. It was quickly absorbed into the fabric of the community and became, through its success, a source of pride for all. Small wonder it came to be regarded as the jewel in the crown of all the social work initiatives of the Craigmillar Festival Society. High praise, indeed.

Our two local councillors, Paul and Davie, fairly basked in its success. In fact, they were the envy of their council chambers colleagues in the Labour Party that controlled Edinburgh at that time. The appeal of the People's College to these politicians was the fact that it was perceived by them as part of that whole Workers Educational Movement which has a long and honourable tradition in Labour politics. This is why at our official opening the person who opened our college, formally, was no less a person than the Labour Lord Provost of the City of Edinburgh himself.

Of course, it goes without saying that, though it was so well received by left-wing politicians for perfectly obvious reasons, there was never anything political about the People's College itself, its atmosphere or its content. We had in our time people of every political opinion, of every religious persuasion, of many cultures and skin tones and, presumably, of all sexualities (I would have no way of knowing, or needing to know).

The local press, that is, the highly regarded national broadsheet, *The Scotsman*, and its local subsidiary, the *Edinburgh Evening News*, virtually ignored us. Even when we were coming to the attention of serious people around Europe and appearing on national television in Britain in the BBC's 'It's my City' competition, which I will tell you about later, they exhibited no interest in our existence.

That said, we almost forced ourselves on their attention in a manner that could have proved very damaging for us, not only reputationally, if things had ended differently in the incident that follows.

Briefly, it was a tradition in the Craigmillar Festival Society that each of its social support arms in turn should periodically undertake to provide a simple lunch for their fellow workers in the community and invited guests. Eventually, our turn arrived. I was nervous but not greatly disheartened by the challenge it presented. When I was getting off the drink a vital part of my self-devised therapy was learning to cook. This took up loads of time: you had to select the menu, do the purchasing and, finally, cook the actual meal. It fitted in with my AA programme of visits and effectively kept me out of trouble. Incidentally, it turned me into quite a good cook (I am being modest here). So, challenging though it was to organise a lunch for over a hundred guests, I welcomed the opportunity to test my culinary skills and stretch them to a new limit.

As usual, working as a collective, the students and I came up with a menu that would be cheap, nutritious and achievable, comprising a main plate of roast chicken breast, a baked potato and salad, served with a sauce of my own invention that I called Shalimar Sauce, which was universally declared to be delicious and much admired. We purchased the ingredients in bulk from a nearby cash-and-carry establishment at trade prices.

Came the day, I gathered my kitchen team around me and explained that everything was to be done with military precision. I showed them a plate with the chicken, baked potato and salad placed in an 'exactly so' position. Each member of the team in turn would have the job of placing their ingredient of the meal on the plates in its precise position (remember, we're talking about over a hundred plates here). I was obsessed with the idea that each guest in the hall next door should face a plate that looked exactly the same as every other plate. Me the masterchef!

Meanwhile, the tension was rising as the guests started to arrive. The heat of the six commercial-sized ovens that were needed was unbearable. This heat and the usual elements of confusion and tomfoolery in my team were driving my stress levels through the roof. Outside in the hall all was going well: the waitressing staff, our female trainees, were slick and proficient and the meal was proving a great success.

It was at this point, with my stress levels stretched to breaking point, that a colleague of mine from the Arts section of the society came into the kitchen and, innocently, said that a reporter from the local press (it was a free meal, after all and the councillors who invited him were political heavyweights) had made the unconsciously flattering but deeply malicious and sarcastic comment that 'that meal must have cost a packet'. He was implying, in his nasty little way, that the money spent on the meal could have been better spent on the training.

When Mike told me this, what with the terrible heat, the stress and the intolerable mean-spiritedness and cheek of it, I completely lost my temper and, in fury, started to push past Mike to get into the hall, crying, "Where is he? Where is he, the bastard! I'll soon sort him out!"

Mike and the rest of my team in the kitchen, greatly alarmed, restrained me physically and held me there by main force till I had calmed down. When I had sufficiently done so, I said to Mike, "All right, I won't go out there but you be sure to tell that snide bastard that that whole meal, dessert included, cost less per person than a single coffee would cost in the swanky Sheriton Hotel that he is never out of, at other people's expense. Tell him that!"

Whether Mike told him this or not, I don't know, but, at least, we didn't get our names in the paper for all the wrong reasons:

LOCAL ACTIVIST ASSAULTS YOUR REPORTER

Let us return to considering the impact of the college on all interested parties. Our superiors on the council staff, who, with one honourable exception in the person of the very supportive Matthew Crighton, had been so aggressively sceptical of our bold initiative from the first, well, they were worn down in the end. I have always lived by that marvellous axiom of Shelley in reference to the Peterloo massacre: 'Look upon them as they slay/Till their rage has died away'.

I don't think that, at the highest levels, for reasons of deep-seated class prejudice, these council officials ever reconciled themselves fully to our high-minded ideas. However, they could not argue with our success and soon found that it was advantageous to capitalise on it.

Thus, we would often be wheeled out at conferences arranged by the council for visiting delegations of notaries from abroad.

I think it may prove illuminating if I were to relate at this point one such conference which has added relevance because it is, on many levels, a shining example of that transformational element that we have just been talking about.

Briefly, this conference, which was being held in the splendid City Council Chambers itself, was addressing social initiatives, including employment issues.

It was a very grand event and welcomed a large number of professionals in the fields of social work and education from Great Britain and abroad.

The council, by this time aware of my abilities as a public speaker, invited me to address this august audience on the subject of my work at the People's College. I was, of course, more than happy to accept any opportunity to talk about my beloved college.

Then, on the very morning of this conference which would take place a few hours later, someone from the council phoned me to ask if it would be possible to bring along a student or two to say a few words.

This posed a considerable problem. First of all, the students were all at that time in their placement phase and spread to the four winds. It wouldn't be easy to find someone who could arrive in the time available. Furthermore, it was, obviously, a big ask to expect a trainee, with no notice of the event, to speak publicly before such an imposing and terrifying group of people.

Then I had a brainwave. Marie Claire! Marie Claire was in many ways the ideal choice. She was in a placement close by at a local primary school, where she was working in the school office. In addition, she was one of the most articulate students we ever had.

But there was, as always, a downside.

Marie Claire had been the victim of a particularly brutal and traumatic experience in her early teens of a sexual nature which had a lasting effect upon her. As a result, she was painfully shy and withdrawn.

To cope with this and, no doubt, the trauma itself she had adopted for herself a mask. She had begun to affect, in her clothes, hair and make-up, a Japanese look. It was skilfully understated, but still very marked. It was strange to look over the class and find what seemed like a beautiful, young geisha with a white-painted face staring back at you. No one in the class took this amiss or even worth commenting on. Marie Claire was simply and unquestioningly accepted for the exotic person she wished herself to be.

How would she react to facing such a daunting audience, looking as distinctive as she did?

How would they react? How would it affect her?

But first of all, would she do it?

I went to her school (it was close by) and explained the situation to her, emphasising that she was my one and only hope. Then, I asked her, rather tentatively, if she would do it. She looked at me with a kind of condescending pity at my hesitancy in asking her. Then she said at once:

"Of course I'll do it. When is it?"

I said, "Well, now actually."

"You mean," said she, "right now, this minute?"

"I'm afraid so," I replied.

"Well, you'll have to give me time to freshen myself up, touch up my make-up."

"No problem," I gratefully replied. "I'll wait for you in the car."

When she appeared, she looked stunning, if a little bizarre, and I was very proud to take her into that exalted company.

Whether on top of the Japanese look she affected, she had acquired some mastery of Zen or not, I do not know. All I can say is that she was the calmest person in that great hall.

When she rose to speak there was an audible gasp of excited interest in the room. She stood, imperious and still, till the room became, again, perfectly silent. Then she spoke. What she produced was a minimalist work of art, a perfect little bonsai of a piece.

She said quite simply, "As a result of being at the People's College, I know who I am and I like who I am."

Then she sat down.

There was a moment of stunned silence, then the hall erupted in wild cheering. What they had just witnessed was nothing less than a 'happening'. It was total theatre. Only I knew that it was entirely unrehearsed and spontaneous.

Marie Claire got a job later as a school secretary. I don't know if she still exhibits her geisha look.

Perhaps she doesn't need it now.

TWENTY-NINE

Interest in our work and the philosophy behind it was, as I have previously stated, scanty to non-existent in Scotland and Great Britain generally. I cannot for the life of me explain this, for, as you will see, interest in the People's College from all parts of Europe was very strong and virtually instantaneous.

It is not as if in some way we targeted Europe. In fact we never at any point or in any way tried to advertise or make public our work to anyone. Yet, significant numbers of people in Europe got to hear about us and, apparently, in Britain no one did.

This is all the more strange in view of the fact that, through no prompting on our part, our name was put forward, presumably by the Edinburgh Council, as an entrant in a BBC-organised competition to discover the best examples in Britain of community work with the disadvantaged.

As a result of this, we appeared several times on national TV. Eventually, we reached the final of this competition and were only pipped at the post by a group working with Caribbean immigrants. So, no shame there.

Despite this national exposure, we had no response from anyone in Britain. As I said, I cannot explain this perverse disregard of our groundbreaking work in Britain when contrasted with the opposite reaction in Europe. However, I am consoled by the fact that it has happened before and to Scottish people of much greater stature and importance than ourselves.

I refer to the great medieval, Franciscan scholar and doctor of the church, Duns Scotus, and David Hume, that shining light of the Scottish Enlightenment.

Both of these intellectual giants were celebrated all over Europe long before being accepted in their own native land of Scotland.

The case of Duns Scotus is particularly striking.

In the Middle Ages he bestrode the European intellectual stage like a colossus and yet, today, few in Scotland, far less Britain, would even know his name. And, yet, ironically, they use it every time they use the word 'dunce'. For the word 'dunce' comes by corruption from 'duns' (meaning 'from Duns', a Scottish Border town and Scotus's birthplace) and was originally a complimentary term to indicate a scholar who had graduated or been 'capped' at a university. In time the word 'dunce' has reversed its original meaning to connote someone who is a failure at school and, therefore, is forced to sit in the corner and wear the dunce's cap of shame.

Perhaps they and we suffered from the same syndrome which in the Bible is encapsulated in the phrase: 'No prophet is recognised in his own country' and in hard-headed Scots is summed up, dismissively, in the phrase: 'Och, ah kent 'es faither'. The implication being that if you knew his father he couldn't be up to much.

Leaving aside tiresome hypotheses concerning this disdain of us at home, it is a relief and pleasure to turn to warm ourselves a little at the fire of European approbation. Irritatingly, I will commence this section thousands of miles away from Europe. In Brazil.

One of the first foreign visitors we had to our college was a social scientist from Brazil who was attending a conference in Glasgow on social disadvantage on behalf of his government. He worked mainly in the *favelas* of Rio de Janeiro and was fascinated to hear at the conference of our work in Craigmillar (how?).

He at once broke off his conference in Glasgow and hurried across country to Edinburgh to spend a couple of hours with us, eagerly soaking up the ways we were endeavouring to turn round great social disadvantage to produce useful members of society as well as free-spirited and confident individuals in their own right. He was absolutely fascinated by our work and by its visible effect on the trainees that he met.

This was the beginning of a contact between us which proved stimulating to both parties. Though, disappointingly, I never got the opportunity to visit Brazil, never got the chance to sink my toes, like some latter-day Robinson Crusoe, in the delectably soft sand of Copacabana Beach.

As time went on, the flock of visitors to our college was regular. They came from universities, colleges, local government organisations, non-governmental organisations and the individually interested. They came from all parts of Europe, from Greece in the east to Portugal in the west and from Scandinavia in the north to the south of France and Italy. The University of the Auvergne used to send us regular batches of undergraduates from their sociology department as part of their scholastic formation.

All were interested in the full range of our work, both social and educational, but undoubtedly the starting point or spur for most of them was our inclusion of cosmology as a major element in our programme of rehabilitation. For some reason the philosophy behind this approach appealed more to the sophisticated European mind. Anyway, they were mad for it and, at times, we were fairly bombarded by their interest.

But, of all the Europeans who showed interest in our work, none came close to the Scandinavians.

One time, when the University of Gothenburg was organising a major conference on social deprivation they invited us to participate. The Edinburgh Council Department concerned refused to authorise the expense for budgetary reasons.

The conference organisers were so anxious for us to appear and talk about our work at the People's College that they insisted on paying all costs, including accommodation, for myself and George Montgomery from my staff to contribute to the conference. The reception of our contribution was enthusiastic and heart-warming and, despite our obscurity and the small scale of our project in a peripheral housing estate in far-off Edinburgh, not in the slightest degree condescending. On the contrary their goodwill towards us and their appreciation of the seriousness of our work gave us great encouragement and made up, to a large extent, for the disappointment we experienced in Great Britain.

But, undoubtedly, our closest friends in Europe were the Danes who deserve a chapter to themselves.

THIRTY

In Denmark at that time, many functions of the state, for example, social work and further education, were run by non-governmental organisations, like the churches and the trade unions.

We had established, I forget how, a contact with a group of enthusiastic trade unionists in Copenhagen who worked mainly with the underprivileged and the unemployed. The affinity between us quickly became a bond and we became more like partners than colleagues, though never in any formal sense. We visited each other's establishments and became friends at all levels. They loved interacting with our students in Craigmillar and our female trainees, in particular, enjoyed the attention of so many handsome and sophisticated Danes.

I will never forget my first visit to Copenhagen. It was, or could have been, intimidating to face a room full of foreigners, even if they all spoke, apparently, perfect English. I said 'could have been' advisedly because it didn't prove so in practice. I fell back on an old oratorical trick

I had used many times in the past: establish personal contact.

So I wrote my full name on the blackboard at the front of the room.

PATRICK McLAUGHLIN

Then I stood back and asked them, "What does that tell you about me?"

They very quickly identified the word 'Patrick' as signifying that I was either Irish or came off Irish people.

I acknowledged the truth of this and then said, "But what about McLaughlin? What do you think that means?"

They all hurried to agree that the 'mac' part meant 'son of', like their 'son' in names such as Larsson or Johannson.

"Yes," I said, "but what about 'laughlin' then?"

They were stumped, which was understandable, and gave up. So, I explained that the 'lin' part stood for 'land'. The 'laugh' element was an Irish variant of 'lough' or 'loch', although in this case it meant not really a loch but a Scandinavian fjord. Thus, 'Patrick McLaughlin' means Patrick, son or descendant of the man from the fjords, or as they say in Ireland, Patrick, son of the Dane. "So," I said, "let's talk as one Viking to another."

From that moment we got on like a house on fire.

I felt sufficiently assured of their empathy to tell them the story of the Battle of Clontarf as told by my old teacher, Andy Powell, which you will remember ended with King Brian Boru and 'two or three of the fellows' overcoming an army of Vikings which was so numerous that their spears were sticking up in the air like fields of waving corn. They all laughed, more than politely; those Danes were nothing if not urbane.

However, the next morning at breakfast when I found myself by chance amongst a small group of our hosts, it became obvious that the story of the Battle of Clontarf had hit a Viking nerve.

One of them said to me, "You know, Pat, that was a wonderful story you told last night of the Battle of Clontarf which, of course, we all know about. However, it wasn't the whole story and misses out a very significant detail. You see, it was the ancient custom of the Vikings to bathe in the sea every Saturday morning, a kind of religious obligation, if you like. This is what they were doing when the Irish fell upon them as they were naked and defenceless in the water."

"Stop there!" I said. "Stop there, if you have any respect for your ancestors. The picture you are presenting of those fearsome Vikings languidly washing and combing their blond locks at the seaside is terribly effeminate and at great odds with their warlike reputation. Had these highly efficient warriors never heard of sentries or lookouts? You would be better to simply admit that on this occasion you got beat and there's an end of it."

This little spat in no way interrupted our growing friendship. In a curious way, it may have enhanced it, for all solid relationships are based on a good deal of give and take.

We were soon to discover that, besides being very genial and warm, our hosts had a tremendous work ethic.

The day following this introduction I have just described, they had prepared for us a full-day programme of visits to the social and educational centres under their control. The programme commenced at 7am (!), when they collected us at our hotel and went on, through several visits to selected venues, to end around 1.30 the next morning (!) when they brought us back to our hotel.

At each of these venues we were entertained to what they call in Danish a *smorrebrod* which is a light buffet of platters of cold meats and artisan cheeses and breads, accompanied by a vast selection of mineral waters and quite exquisite coffee.

At the end of the day, what with the great amount of food taken and the intensive nature of the schedule, we were exhausted, especially as they insisted on taking us on a tour of the city after dinner at one of the poshest restaurants in Copenhagen.

At one point, when we were totally spent and in need of matchsticks to keep our eyes open, they pointed out to us in the distance the tomb of King Olaf the Great or some such royal celebrity. Their enthusiasm could not be faulted but, in truth, we could see nothing of the tomb because it was pitch-dark at the time and between us and the tomb there was an intervening apartment block.

Their dedication to the task and passionate enthusiasm went a long way to explaining why their Viking forebears were so successful in their expansion and their conquests around the turn of the first millennium AD.

When it came our turn to reciprocate their hospitality some time later in Edinburgh, we had real apprehensions about our ability to match the wonderful experience they had provided for us in Denmark.

I decided to make a virtue of necessity. Instead of a rigorous and tight schedule of events and entertainments, such as we had experienced in Denmark, I constructed a more skeletal programme with deliberate gaps in it to allow them the opportunity to sample the delights of Edinburgh. It could have seemed a bit of a cop-out on our part but I'm glad to say that they did not regard it in this light. They loved the freedom it gave them to wander at will in the beautiful city of Edinburgh and always returned to us buoyant and refreshed.

The catering at the People's College was a major headache. How could we provide a lunch anything like the wonderful buffets we had enjoyed in Copenhagen?

Here the local councillors came to our aid. Through them, we managed to book the official caterers of the city council to provide lunch! These caterers were used to hosting guests of the highest calibre, including international politicians and royalty. Surely they would be more than a match, even for those lovely Danish *smorrebrods*?

And I am sure they would have been, if it weren't for the fact that the very day before the event, the caterers informed us that, due to a double booking, they would not be able to provide their services.

This was, not to put too fine a point on it, a devastating blow for us. How could we possibly fill this gap in our hospitality?

Then, David Hamilton, the ex-miner who was on our staff at the time, suggested that we get the Danderhall Miners' Club to provide a 'purvey', as it was called.

A purvey was a couple of boards of pies, sausage rolls, sandwiches and cakes that were provided cheaply by the Miners' Club for funerals and parties in working-class communities. The fare was rustic, to say the least: the pies, called Scotch pies, ran with grease and the sandwich rolls looked as if they had been cut with an axe.

We were thoroughly mortified at the very idea of presenting this kind of rough fare to our ultra-sophisticated guests.

In the event, our Danish friends, to whom a purvey was a total novelty, loved it and kept singing the praises of this miners' club purvey for a long time afterwards, even when back in Denmark. I suppose it is comparable to the appeal of 'a bit of rough' to a sophisticated and refined sexual palate. They commented on its great superiority to the food provided at the high-class restaurant to which we took them for their evening meal. One person said – and he wasn't drunk at the time – that the restaurant meal was good of its type but couldn't hold a candle to the People's College.

THIRTY-ONE

Now we are approaching the last and climactic act of our little drama. We have traced the growth of a bold, but simple idea of transforming, by means of education, the lives of numbers of individuals from a reviled and deprived neighbourhood; through its development in detailed practice; to its apotheosis in the steady progress of so many into meaningful employment and settled and fulfilling lives.

We witnessed the journey of the pioneers of this concept, myself and the co-creating Craigmillar community, as we, together, overcame disdain, opposition and indifference to achieve widespread fame and reputation well beyond our gates.

The most celebrated and contentious element in this concept was our inclusion of a course on cosmology.

The whole idea of using cosmology in the way we did, to transform lives, was certainly eye-catching, as has been seen, but much more important was its centrality to everything we were trying to achieve in our little community in the People's College. The fundamental significance of cosmology to our project could not be overstated. It was the foundation of everything that we did; it coloured everything, shaped it and gave it life. Take cosmology out of the equation and our whole enterprise would have fallen flat on its face like some dangling marionette when someone cuts its string.

The intriguing question is: 'Where did this big idea come from?'.

It certainly didn't emerge directly or obviously from my own study of cosmology. Though my reading in the field was extensive, nowhere in all of the thousands upon thousands of words I read on the subject had I found even a hint of how it could be used in this way.

If I had, I would have been most happy to embrace the hint and, after due acknowledgement, I would have made it my own, making it serve my own formative purposes. In this respect I would be merely following the sage advice of the great Duns Scotus himself who famously said, 'Heed not by whom a thing is said but, rather, what is said take to your heart'. What is important is the thought, not the conceiver of the thought.

However, strictly for the record, this didn't happen. I never found anywhere a ready-made recipe for using cosmology to reorder lives and change perspectives in the way that we did.

The idea came to me, all unlooked for, in a flash of inspiration or, as the cliché has it, in a light-bulb moment. But, like all seemingly random events in life, it was not all that random. On the contrary, it was in reality the result of a lifetime of prior experiences, decisions, choices, twists and turns, highs and lows, coincidences and consequences that it would take a book to explain. (This is that book.)

At all events, when the idea of using cosmology in this particular way did come to pass, it was something that I felt was normal, natural, even inevitable in a kind of a way. It did not occur to me that it could be groundbreaking and original in some more historic sense.

Then something happened that changed all that.

Unbeknownst to me, a noted academic at one of the most prestigious seats of learning in Germany was setting out to make a name for himself in a particular field of cosmology with strong links to the arts and humanities that he was claiming for his own. To this end, he published an article in a prestigious academic journal outlining his ideas.

This article fell into the hands of a member of the academic staff at Edinburgh University. He at once noticed, or thought he did, some similarities with my own work on cosmology in Craigmillar. He photocopied the article and gave it to a mutual friend on the Edinburgh Council staff to pass on to me.

When I read it, I honestly could not see much resemblance between my work and the theory outlined in the learned article. The writer of that essay was, as it were, writing in high Latin in one of the ivory towers of academe, while I, by contrast, was sitting outside my tent in the desert, making simple marks in the sand with a stick.

However, there was an unmistakable concomitance in the basic ideas. This was reinforced by the fact that I, entirely unused to the notoriously dense and tortuous language of academic papers, was able to read and understand it without too much difficulty. Perhaps – and I am aware that I am making a big leap here – this was because there was something not altogether unfamiliar in the ideas proposed.

Reading it, I felt as if I was desperately trying to manoeuvre a canoe through the dangerously choppy rapids of a very fast-flowing river. But a river that I had the vague sense of having been in before. No more than that.

On impulse, I wrote to the professor concerned and explained to him about my modest endeavours in the field of cosmology.

I had previously published an explanatory article on our cosmology programme in our in-house newsletter, *The Collegian*, which I told you about before. I enclosed with my letter a copy of this newsletter, containing the article in question.

Subsequently, I received a hastily handwritten letter of reply from him in which he thanked me for sending him the piece about cosmology. He said he found it of much interest and that he felt it deserved a fuller critique on his part which he promised to provide as soon as he was back at his desk. He apologised for this delay and explained that he was in an airport lounge between flights at the time of writing.

I was very pleased with this reply and flattered that such a highly placed academic would undertake to correspond with me.

I showed it joyfully to my wife. She read it through and then threw it down dismissively on the table in front of me and said, "Put it in the bin. That's the last you'll hear of that man. Too busy to write just now? Catching a plane? Give me a break! It's the kiss-off, the classic Dear John, if ever I saw one."

"Hold on a minute," I blurted out. "He has promised to send me a critique of my article. So, he must be taking my work seriously. Surely, that is clear enough!"

"Mark my words, you have made an enemy of that man. And I can tell you why, if you wish."

"Perhaps you'd better, dear, for it sure beats the hell out of me," I crustily replied.

"Do you remember," she said, "a previous conversation we had about the groundbreakers in science? The ones who discovered something startling that changed the course of history. Like Copernicus who became famous for discovering that Earth and the other planets went round the sun, rather than the other way round."

"Well, to be truthful," I interjected, "he wasn't the first person to have that idea. The theory of the heliocentric Solar System was in the air. It was already being talked about in scientific circles."

"Of course it was," she admitted. "But the point is that he was the first to publish the theory and, thus, put his name to it. This is why we call it the Copernican Revolution and not something else. Then there was yer man, Darwin. Didn't you tell me that he nearly lost out on being called the father of evolution?"

"Yes," I confidently replied. "On analogy with Copernicus, he wasn't the only one to come up with the idea of natural selection or survival of the fittest being the prime mover of evolution. At around that time there were others, including, notably, Patrick Matthew and Alfred Russel Wallace, who had published exploratory papers on the subject. But the greatest danger to Darwin was posed by Wallace who was on the verge of publishing his fully fleshed-out theory of evolution. If he had managed to do so, he would have become the founder of evolution, rather than Darwin. Aware of this, Darwin pushed on at neck-break speed to get his great work, *On the Origin of Species*, published first. It is proof that he managed to do so that today we refer to Darwin's Theory of Evolution rather than Wallace's."

"Precisely," my wife persisted, "in science to be the first to publish, is all. Nobel Prizes are based on this. Now, look at the beginning of his article in the journal that was passed on to you. Unless my memory fails me, doesn't he say there when his interest in this new field of cosmology first started?"

I scrambled to find the reference.

"Here it is," I said, triumphantly. "Yes, in 1979. That's when he said that his interest in the subject first began."

My wife, still ominously subdued, said, "Now look at the date on the college newsletter that you sent him describing your own work in the field. What does it say?"

I read the date at the top of the page of *The Collegian*... March 1976!

"So, your actual work on this topic was ongoing and successful before he even sat down to think about it. And he now knows it! Can't you see how that would drive him up the wall?"

I squirmed. "But you know very well, dear, that there is no real comparison between his magnificently articulated work and my few scribblings in the field."

"Yes, but what scribblings!" she triumphantly exclaimed. "The germ of the idea is clearly there in your work. And in your work it is not merely an academic theory but something concrete and realised. It is as if he had hypothesised about building a spacecraft to take man to the moon only to discover that you were already commuting there on a regular basis. Or, to put it another way, it is as if Einstein were to subsequently discover that some unknown graffiti artist had been going around scrawling the mysterious and apparently random formula, $E=mc^2$, on the walls of public buildings years before he developed and published his groundbreaking Theory of General Relativity whose critical nub is this very formula.

"Can't you see how that would upset him? You have tarnished the professor's work in his own eyes. You've ruined it for him. To be playing catch-up to one of your peers in academia is bad enough, but to be doing so to a simple classroom teacher in a working-class backwater is an intolerable thought. You have become a threat to his reputation. Without the slightest doubt you have seen – or rather, heard – the last of that man."

And so it was.

Subsequently, in the years that followed, we went on to find continuing success in our efforts to mend broken lives and to further faltering dreams. Meanwhile our fame, based mainly on our cosmological component, spread through Europe and beyond.

As for the professor, we never heard of him again.

EPILOGUE

Nothing lasts forever. One fateful day the People's College and all it stood for came to an end and closed its doors for the last time.

It did not fail because of any perceived failure on its part to do the job it was designed to do. Neither did it come to an end because the need for it no longer existed. No, the People's College ended purely and simply as a result of a cold, bureaucratic decision taken far away from Craigmillar in the upper echelons of the European Union.

Consequent on the expansion of the European Community to include very impoverished Eastern European countries, it became necessary to review priorities in the distribution of funds under the tight European Social Fund budget. As a result of this review Scotland, with the exception of the Highlands and Islands, no longer qualified for social fund assistance and, so, our enterprise was deprived of any contribution from Europe.

The People's College could not survive this crushing blow to our finances.

There was no way in the world that the Edinburgh City Council would be able to make up the deficit. Local governments are notoriously hard-pressed for money and the funds needed to plug this gap in our finances would have been significant. It was simply out of the question. Furthermore, there was no possible alternative source of funding, no improbable capitalist sugar daddy who, on a whim, would pump money into our venture.

No, our fate was effectively and permanently sealed across a table that day in Brussels and there was nothing we could do about it.

In its startling abruptness our demise mirrored in miniature the extinction of the dinosaurs 67 million years ago. These magnificent and eminently viable creatures had dominated the planet for an astonishing 165 million years and yet they disappeared from the face of the earth in the cosmological blink of an eye.

This was not due to any evolutionary or otherwise fault in their design. It was not, as some of the sillier theories have it, because they had grown too big for their boots and could no longer support the weight of their ever more massive bodies. Evolution just doesn't work like that; it doesn't select for failure. That would make no sense. Evolution does not have a self-destructive reverse gear. On the contrary, it selects exclusively in favour of those best adapted to survive and propagate themselves. Its motto is always, 'onwards and upwards!'.

Secondly, it should be said that not all dinosaurs were massive; some, on the contrary, were quite small.

Lastly, any putative flaw or inherent defect in the constitution of the dinosaurs would have taken a very long period of time to pass down the generations and thus lead to the species dying out. Certainly eons. And yet, from the geological record, we know, for sure, that the dinosaurs disappeared, geologically speaking, almost overnight.

So, what did happen to the dinosaurs?

There is strong evidence to suggest that what caused their disappearance was an incursion from outer space, for example, an asteroid or comet or, perhaps, a meteorite no bigger than a football field. When it struck the earth, the thermonuclear explosion that resulted wreaked devastation over a large area of the earth's surface. It also caused to rise up and permeate the atmosphere a vast and impenetrable cloud of dust, debris, carbon dioxide and sulphur that blocked off all the light from the sun and brought about an unnatural arctic winter all over the planet.

As a result of this cataclysm, 96% of all species on Earth and in the sea, including the dinosaurs, perished. *Sic transit gloria mundi.*

At least it could be said that the magnificent dinosaurs, one of the glories of the world, did not end with a whimper but a bang – and then some!

Some small, furry mammals had managed to escape this extinction event because they were protected from its consequences by finding themselves in warm crevices in rocks deep under the surface of the earth. After the devastation, these tiny creatures emerged, blinkingly, from their secure little lairs in the rocks to populate the empty world and, so, produce the Age of Mammals of which we humans are the crowning achievement.

However, even a civilisation as advanced as ours is always living precariously, on a knife edge you might say. This is because the threat of another annihilation is always hanging over us. At any moment a rogue asteroid or a comet from the Van Oort belt could strike the earth and produce another mass extinction.

But a more likely, though equally fatal, theory suggests that our destruction will be self-induced. Computer simulations made by scientists who work in the field of futurology or predictive science have prognosticated that an advanced civilisation, such as ours, will always end up by destroying itself.

It is not all that difficult to see how, in our modern world, that threat is not only immanent, but imminent. With the proliferation of nuclear weapons and no end of madmen in control of them, there is a very real possibility that the world could stumble at any moment into a nuclear war which could lead to the extinction of all life on Earth.

Even if that were to be avoided, there is the ever-present menace posed by global warming. Once global warming reaches a certain tipping point – and this is terribly close, if it hasn't already been reached – it will become irreversible and lead to consequences that could spell the end of all life on Earth.

Due to the rampant destruction of the carbon-capturing rainforests, when allied to the mass-release of carbon, hitherto locked up safely and harmlessly for millions of years in the bowels of the earth, we are changing and destabilising the planetary weather system. We can see this happening on a global scale around us every day. The process of global warming which results from the increase of carbon in the atmosphere has been going on for some time now but is undoubtedly accelerating, as I have explained in an earlier part of this book. Soon it will pose a threat to all life on Earth by making the planet uninhabitable.

Perhaps this is why the scientific community is spending so much time, effort and resources on space exploration. Ostensibly they are exploring the cosmos, and in particular our nearest neighbours in the Solar System, in the scientific pursuit of knowledge for its own sake.

However, I am sure that it is not too far from the minds of the governments concerned that, at some time in the future, human life will only be possible, at least for an elite, if we can manage to escape our doom by creating colonies on some hospitable, neighbouring planet.

At this point I am struck by how prescient were those tough, young school-underachievers in St Patrick's all those years ago with their space play, *The Second Chance*, that I told you about earlier in this work.

But would there be, or could there be, a second chance for the People's College?

It is easy to see how there could not be. The original concept and its carrying out to full fruition depended very heavily on the vision, personal history, aptitudes and skills of one particular individual. Furthermore, this strongly academically-based initiative depended utterly on its unquestioning and wholehearted acceptance by an unlikely group of down trodden individuals with a background of deprivation at all levels, societal, cultural and educational. That it turned out to be such a great success was a tribute to the fact that, by great good luck, the ordinary people of Craigmillar proved themselves to be anything but ordinary in their resilience, open-mindedness and good-natured optimism.

There was a lot of good fortune involved in achieving that perfect balance. To manage to replicate that result would require an immense number of ducks to be lined up in the exquisitely right order. This is a very tall order. No, an exact replication of the People's College is not at all foreseeable in any future that could be imagined. The phenomenon that was the People's College was a one-off and it is gone.

However, in all extinction scenarios, of which there have been at least three in the history of the planet that we know about, there is always a scintilla of hope. Someone or something always survives. These survivors, be they microbial or complex organisms, develop in ways that are totally unpredictable and push evolution in entirely new, and sometimes antithetical, directions.

Whatever form the People's College manages to take after the cataclysm of its demise, it will not be as before. The only thing to be hoped for is that greater awareness of its success, and the key ideas that underpinned that success, may stimulate interest in the concept. If even one of those ideas takes root in some mind, it could bud out in some unimaginable way to produce something entirely new and no less significant.

It would still carry in its DNA the memory of the People's College, as water is said by the proponents of homeopathy to carry the health-giving memory of some tincture or infusion that has been added to it, even after every physical particle of the original infusion has been eliminated following multiple dilutions.

Who knows, this very book itself may provide the vehicle for this survival.

It is possible that some unknown reader may be touched or inspired by it and roused to respond to its challenge. If so, this book, with all its messiness and frequent digressions, could be imagined, to pursue the cosmological metaphor, as being like a characteristically spindly-looking space probe. (Since there is no advantage in the near-vacuum of space to having an aerodynamic contour, space probes have a typically inelegant and even cluttered appearance with all their antennae, tools and other pieces of scientific equipment stuck on the outside. This is why a typical deep-space vehicle resembles less a Japanese bullet train than the tool-laden burro of a Californian gold-prospector.)

Still, it gets the job done and that's all that matters.

The most we can hope for is that our imagined little spacecraft can also do the job for us as it bleep-bleeps its way into the vast unknowingness of the future in the wild hope of contacting, or being contacted by, some redemptive intelligence that would ensure the survival of the concept – in whatever new form that survival takes.

If this colossally unlikely outcome were to be realised there may yet be a second chance for the People's College.

If so, it would be only fitting for an organisation that was the offspring of more than one second chance and dispensed second chances to other unfortunates with the deftness of a professional card-dealer.

Long live the second chance!

This book is printed on paper from sustainable sources managed under the Forest Stewardship Council (FSC) scheme.

It has been printed in the UK to reduce transportation miles and their impact upon the environment.

For every new title that Matador publishes, we plant a tree to offset CO_2, partnering with the More Trees scheme.

For more about how Matador offsets its environmental impact, see www.troubador.co.uk/about/